The *Wandering Jew*

my personal search for Jewish identity

MILTON FIRMAN

Dedicated to the memory of every single human being of whatever religion, race, ethnic group or sexual persuasion who so tragically and needlessly perished at the hands of the Nazi regime

This book is also a lasting tribute to my dear father Jack Firman (formerly Jacob Fireman) who was, and will always be, my hero

INTRODUCTION

"Some people like the Jews, and some do not. But no thoughtful man can deny the fact that they are, beyond any question, the most formidable and the most remarkable race which has appeared in the world."

- WINSTON CHURCHILL

It is a sunny September afternoon as I wander almost like an automaton among a multitude of gravestones precariously positioned on bumpy ground.

This is Phillips Park Cemetery near Phillips Park in Whitefield, a few miles north of Manchester, where my father was buried on the 14th February 1979 about twenty four hours after he had tragically died, drawing the final curtain on a relatively short but precious life. He left a wife and two children. Lost. Totally and utterly lost.

It is now just before the Jewish New Year, as I delicately tiptoe among these tombstones bearing names, pondering the thin line between the life of the living and what might possibly lie beyond. This is without doubt a perfectly awful place, even in the brightest of sunshine.

I drag my heels in the mud as I recall with freezing horror that fateful day – 13th February 1979, when my life was blown apart and I was so mercilessly robbed of my best friend and my mentor - my father. Aged a mere twenty-five, I felt deprived - and so I was. As I now read, on an upright slab of cold granite, the name of '***Jack Firman***' I am like a lost orphan boy searching for meaning – yet well over 30 years later. Only more recently have I fully appreciated what my loss truly represented when I turn for advice, but dad isn't at home any longer. His experience of life swept away like the outgoing tide - leaving just pebbles on the shore.

We were both far too young to lose one another's company so soon. We were separated forever and yet only now, so many years later, do I fully appreciate the extent and the true impact of my loss. Only in adulthood do I get to know my father intimately, having experienced more of life myself. But it is far too late to say goodbye and impossible to retrospectively ask the unanswered questions that dawn on me with the benefit of maturity.

This is a place of such absolute desolation and finality. I know full well that we must all lose our fathers one day - unless of course they tragically lose us first. This is one of life's absolutes – a mere truism. But I do wonder how little I could have really known my father by the time he left me when he did. He had never heard of Tony Blair or John Major and the creation of the Internet meant nothing to my dad. He was fond of the Beatles and even Rod Stewart's '***Sailing***,' loved Nat King Cole but really despised pickled herring. It is all like yesterday. I can visualise my father's veined, piano-playing hands in my mind's eye with people gathered around him in awe as his fingers skipped along the ivory keys. I remember feeling immensely proud as he played the next melody with his usual consummate ease. I would beam with pride as I watched him conduct the choir at our synagogue just up the road from where he now lies. He was in command, and was terribly good at it - even though I may say so myself.

When I was young, these thoughts did not really cross my mind but now they seem to engulf me like a tsunami. The inside of my head is swirling in the eerie silence of this desolate cemetery where life as we know it ceases to exist, at a stroke. There is solitude mingled only with desperation and pointlessness. This is not a joyous place, and the stillness screams at me. The utter loneliness echoes in my eardrums as if I am incarcerated in an endless tunnel.

I once knew this particular Jewish community intimately, but all I witness now are the fragments of the past laid bare in this neglected, greyish and haunting parkland. The only breathing I can hear is my own. I hesitate at the gravestone of a newly born child whose family I know so well, and whose grieving and wailing I can still hear resounding in my ears. These are memories I want to wash away like the mud off my shoe, but these recollections cling to me as an intrinsic part of who I am.

I soon shudder with fright as I come to a sudden and abrupt halt beside a tombstone that commemorates an innocent teenager whose life was tragically and prematurely ended by his own disturbed and troubled mind. I reflect upon how grieving parents can wake up each morning without the sight of their fresh-faced offspring's reassuring and youthful smile. I recently hear that this once-young man's own father had himself died and I am touched by profound sadness. There is stillness. The birds don't dare to sing in this lonely place. They find a happier location where life carries on - apparently undaunted. This is not a place for pleasant melodies, but rather more for serious and composed expressions of grief.

I then begin to pray inside my confused head for the pretty young girl who whilst at university was mercilessly mowed down by a drunken driver. I think about such an unimaginably painful loss to her devoted parents who surely can never entirely recover from such horror that must amount to the absolute tragedy. I stumble. I am helpless. I have no words of comfort to offer up to her - poor thing. I am heartbroken for such needless loss and I stand in respectful silence as if rather naively, it might make some small difference. These are some of life's horror stories laid bare. One just thinks who and what might have been.

I even mull over the fate of the offending driver and his own private thoughts of reflection and regret – hopefully some guilt and some soul-searching, though I will never find out. I cry alone, but I cry real tears that I shyly mop up with my crumpled tissue that I brought with just in case, and which I clumsily pull from my trouser pocket. Forearmed - as they say. This is a place for tears. If not here, where? Memories, so many memories. Reflections. Regrets. Reminiscences.

I am speechless as I wander utterly absorbed in my own personal and cluttered space. I feel the tempo of an entire Jewish congregation pulsating in the pervading silence. I walk around aimlessly and haphazardly shuffling along a random route, and finding some mild, if not perverse, solace in reading and recalling familiar names whilst in my semi-frozen daze. I am like a stone – transfixed. Immoveable. Rigid. Almost like granite itself.

I soon mouth to myself the words that are scrawled in felt tip pen on a piece of off-white card that has been deliberately speared into a clump of grubby soil nearby, and I jolt forward. I see that it bears the name of a former school friend who was in stature large but, at far too tender an age, has been swept away by the ravages of life itself. Having died a few months earlier, he is patiently waiting his turn to have his very own tombstone unveiled (an accolade he sadly will never live to see.) I cannot help but consider what a pathetic and anonymous ending this is for him and for all of us. Life has seemingly been blown away in the autumn breeze whilst life appears to carry on elsewhere - unmoved, untouched, almost undaunted. A life wafted away like a wasp or a bumblebee.

I can feel the tingle of another lukewarm tear gathering momentum as it drips down my cheek as I privately dwell upon Jeremy's endearing and jovial manner. I am absurdly hoping that he is not feeling any pain right now, and I even dare to dream of him being somewhere better. I dream. I hope. I stand by - and I reminisce about happier and more boisterous times when life was life for Jeremy, and not dumped in a pit.

Though this is not a place for laughter, I allow myself the luxury of smiling to myself unnoticed as I think of our school days together at Stand Grammar, as if it were all happening yesterday, because in a sense it seems to me right now as if it actually is. Time moves on and yet it stands still. Time here is never - and yet forever; the clock has stopped ticking. 'Tick-tock-tick'. The disorderly rows of stonemasonry don't offer any answers or any real consolation for me as all these lives around me are extinguished.

I crave for any underlying and enduring purpose to all this chaos. I cry out for meaning to this nonsense. Life transformed to sand, and life's journey universally wiped away like chalk off the school board.

I wander along a few rows more and then stand stoically next to my grandparents' gravestones – accompanying one another in death as in life and whose stones are seriously weatherworn by the passing years. I take a moment out for my uncle Harry, who died young and is perchance in the same unkempt row two or three away. I tragically spot some vacant ground adjacent to his gravestone, and my thoughts turn to auntie Terri* who, now in her 90s, has cancer and who is doubtless destined to occupy that particular plot, though hopefully in the far distant future. It has, I gather, been 'reserved' for the inevitable, whenever that shall be. Once a Tiller girl and a high-kicking dancer, my aunt finds it difficult to even stand up nowadays. Once again, I wonder to myself where the intervening years have gone, and where we are all ultimately running to. I recognise that sadly there is destined to be no more dancing for Terri as those days are well and truly over. I reflect upon the inevitability of old age, what it brings, and what it takes away. Its happiness, its despair and its inevitability. The many things we took for granted.

There are too many unspoken words this day. My mind is full to overflowing and my malaise compelling. I wander around aimlessly - touched by what I see as well as the illusions my mind creates in order to help me ease my pain. There is definitely no singing here - neither the birds nor me. We are stunned into respectful silence. Time to think. Time to wonder and desperate for answers. The weeds. The stones. The words. The remoteness.

To say that this place brings me thoroughly ***down to earth*** is both metaphorically and literally true. The deathly silence stops me perfectly in my tracks, as I stand alone - immersed in my own personal whirlwind of confusion. This is a desperate place where life ceases, where time is terminated at random, and my own heart races - I hear its beating inside my chest. I imagine, in my more pretentious moments, that I am full of spirituality, in my frantic search for a more profound explanation for this sheer emptiness and echoing vacuum.

But I also feel undeniably and quintessentially Jewish among all these gravestones as every single tombstone marks the spot where a Jew once lived - but no more. Some of these Jewish men and women were religious, others were secular, but all, every solitary one of them, were by birth and certainly in death, Jewish. And now they are part of a newly created community, one that celebrates the past, but one that lives only in the memory. Until that memory in due course will doubtless fade too as each generation creates its own picture book. Even the fondest memories are not destined to be eternal. This is the price of mortality.

And so here lies my extended family. This is the bond that connects each of these building blocks – a testimony to the wandering Jew, and those Jews who wander no more including my father, my maternal grandparents and my uncle Harry. These are the people who define who I am. These are the Israelites, the Wandering Jews, who rose from slavery, oppression, the pogroms and well-ingrained anti-Semitism, to stand proud as Jews. The survivors. Until they were to perish too - as we all are destined to do one day. And the cemetery grew and grew, and in due course the survivors who were bound to succumb to mortality lie here silently, inconspicuously and helplessly. This is a place that will only close its doors when full to capacity one day in the long distant future.

Even death cannot wipe away my tears. We Jews are born to be Jews and, like the tide, we might ebb and flow, but most of us inevitably and eventually return to the place with which we are innately familiar. We return home to the home of our people. Whether running to synagogue on the High Holy Days, wandering around a cemetery as I'm doing, reminiscing about Jewish lives past and present, or lighting the memorial candle on the anniversary of a loved one's demise, we return - because this is who we are. And this is what Jews have always done and do now.

It only feels like yesterday when my grandparents appeared immortal to their dutiful grandson, and yet all I am left with nowadays are a few cracked photographs, a worn but legible Russian Passport, some postcards from the Isle of Man Internment Camp, and fading memories lodged somewhere in my flickering imagination. What purpose? What meaning? What difference? Who has made (or indeed will ever make) our true and lasting mark in this vast but shrinking world? What is our true legacy? These are just some of the myriad questions swirling around in my overloaded head. The cemetery is by its very nature a catalyst to some extremely serious contemplation and much profound reflection upon the true meaning of life. Death right now puts life in its most stark perspective.

One day it might be someone else's duty to remember me, but today I bring to the forefront of my mind my maternal grandpa, Eli Knoll, formerly of Toporov in Poland, a very good looking man even in old age who could often be seen walking proudly as he was strutting briskly to synagogue dressed in his tailored suit and immaculate, crisp white shirt and tie. He came from one of the **shtetls*** where I like to imagine Jews looked after one another, probably because they all had little material wealth and capitalism having thankfully not engulfed them just yet. Like so many before and after him, he was a tailor and soon learned to sell his wares to farmers in the Yorkshire countryside, driving his car without ever having passed a driving test but somehow rather miraculously getting there nevertheless.

I recall my childhood visits to Heywood Road in Prestwich, where grandma and grandpa lived and where I ate fig biscuits from a battered biscuit tin bearing, if my memory serves me correctly, a scene of Skipton no less. My grandma Sarah, now Knoll but formerly Isaacs, was the archetypal Jewish matriarch, dutiful, strong and fiercely loyal, whilst my grandfather believed that he was in control, though he probably rarely was. I purposely pass by their house from time to time to recall days when as a child I searched for four leaved clovers with real anticipation. These were, as I remember them now, splendid days of innocence and timelessness. These were the distant days of walnut wardrobes, Bakelite telephones and a wrestler popular at the time, by the name of Mick McManus, faking every single fall onto the canvas, on a Saturday afternoon's black and white TV screen. Grandpa was glued to it when the wrestling came on as he hadn't turned *frum** yet. He was in no doubt that each of the falls was genuine, though I tried to convince him otherwise. It made him happy and so I gave up trying. Best not to be too cynical.

For me life went on forever, as I had no perception of time unerringly ticking by. There was no hurry at all in those days, as I was not planning to grow old. That was for others but definitely not for me. I was young and old age didn't touch me.

In the cemetery today, as if I need reminding, I see how wrong I was. That life is short - very short, especially when looking back over the course of many years. Time used to canter but now it is galloping away just like a horse free from its reins. I try to run after it and gather it in my palm, but with no success at all.

For the cemetery visit, I dutifully wear my *yarmulke** as a small token of my respect to the Almighty should He really be out there after all. I am also aware that my Jewish heritage is at the very epicentre of my visit to this chilly place. Something intangible beats in my heart, as I return to my roots. Here is my link to a rich yet troubled past. Though I am distraught in these degrading and dingy surroundings, I nevertheless feel curiously proud of the unbroken Jewish connection of which I am a miniscule part.

As I meander among these pitiful and rigid monuments to silence, I am also confused by my mixed emotions of pride and despair. It is as if I am **lost and yet found**. This might indeed be the true message of my own, my very personal observation, this particular Milton's **Paradise Lost**. But this is definitely no paradise, though I might well be lost. I certainly have an insatiable appetite for the answers that I seek, but which I have to date failed miserably to find. I am the lost child looking for his daddy, though knowing full well that I have nil chance of finding him here today, or even tomorrow.

In the less than auspicious surroundings of Whitefield Cemetery, it is therefore as if I have **returned home** – to familiar names and to a community of which I remain an integral part and memories of those youthful carefree days that I remember with genuinely animated delight. I walk into the Prayer Room, where I stand respectfully for a few detached moments, possibly in search of my own personal renewal and a moment of inspiration. I look for truth in the self-reflection of silence and against the background of richly coloured stained glass windows. They add a strange tinge of brightness to an otherwise cold interior. I can touch the stillness. I can feel my inner-self. I am numb, powerless. I listen to ensure my heart is still beating. The cold tiled floor epitomises the lack of adornment and the deliberately clinical surroundings that somehow befit such a place as this. When a funeral takes place here, there can be a throng of people milling around, but today I am alone in this empty room with its grandiose windows projecting a coloured reflection onto the blackness of the floor tiles.

A few moments later and I am walking away with a certain turbulent introspection down a sharpish incline to my car parked nearby, just beyond the gates and where life **busies** itself - apparently oblivious to the silent ones - out of sound. Life is now as it was before beyond the gates of the deathly silence that I have just been listening to. A silence that speaks loudly and profoundly to me and yet does not stop the world outside going about its routine business. Like on a theatrical stage, the show goes on.

I depart head bowed out of some misguided sense of respect for those who cannot talk to me. I am full of melancholy but grateful to be walking away. I have learned over time to be thankful. The sun shines down on some random bushes at the side of the tarmac path, and I marvel at nature's on-going and seasonal magic, the source of which I am unable to explain.

The Jewish custom is to place a single stone on the gravestone of our loved ones on each visit, though we don't generally place flowers at the graveside. The stone we leave, I was once misled, represents the rock God is. On my visit today, I leave a stone at several gravesides as a gesture towards each person I once knew, but whose life has ended. I want each one of them to know that I have not forgotten them and that I have paid them a visit. The thought of them being alone makes me shudder. Loneliness can be painful in life, and so it must surely be in death too.

I notice wild and wispy weeds growing in abundance and wonder what their purpose might be. This is not a resting place for the living but for the dead, and the weeds tell their own story of neglect and disarray, somehow embellishing the scene of sadness. This is a location where the only colour is darkness – and where tragedy only speaks in silence. It all represents an uncompromising finality and epitomizes, if no more, the final journey on this earth as we know it.

There is nothing to do in this wretched place other than to wander, as I have done many times before and will do again - to think and to pray - that there may hopefully be more to life than this unspoken and indiscriminate lottery. That unjust will become just and that sadness will again wear a happy smile, and that life will even be re-born in some form or other in another place and on another day. I think to myself that I must leave room in my heart for just one thing: **Hope**. I need to hope that there is more than this ending, and that a new and fresh beginning beckons somewhere, some place, some time. I urge myself never to lose that **Hope**, but we shall see. I shall go in search.

I come to this cemetery from time to time not only because I feel obliged to do so but also because I am drawn here. I find great solace in walking around and somehow respecting those who have left for pastures new. In my heart I know only too well that I am not able to communicate with the dead, but only with myself. There is a vast array of the fondest memories to rekindle and as I navigate between the graves I think of God who remains such a mystery. I wonder why He would choose to put us through this protracted purgatory. I am always at a total loss to understand why. If there were ever a perfect place to sell the 'Big Issue', it would surely be right here right now, as this is where the fundamental, philosophical conundrums need unwinding and unravelling in order to reveal an answer or two.

I ponder to myself that if He revealed Himself to Moses, then why not to me? I am perplexed and have no answers. I am obsessed by this recurring sense of futility and a begrudging acceptance that nothing appears to last forever.

As I leave my father, I feel like a cheat, deserting him yet again, as if patronising him with my token gestures and my crocodile tears. I have strategically placed down another stone to keep him company, which I position prominently and proudly, in order to let the whole world know how special my father is to me. Yet once down the hill and round the corner onto Park Lane, I will be turning up the volume on Radio 4 and the cemetery will be no more than a faint figment memory. Until my next visit.

I am, as I have just admitted, well aware that I have found some small element of selfish comfort in *returning home*. Divested of worldly possessions, a cemetery like this one, with its weathered stone masonry and its faded lettering, is destined to be my eternal resting place one day. I am only a few spades of dirty, black, soggy earth away. I am transfixed for a moment or two. The line is so thin, the journey so tenuous, life itself so alarmingly brief. It is only time that divides us.

When I was a youngster I thought that I knew it all, but now I know nothing with any absolute certainty. I used to be dogmatic, and yet nowadays I am dithering. Things used to be black and white and yet, as an adult, they are predominantly grey, just like those rows of granite. I do not know anymore what it is that I do not know - but I admit what little I know. I suspect that this admission is a sign of growing old. This cemetery is the lasting proof that there is only one thing worse than growing old and that is - *not* growing old.

I leave the cemetery but I shall be returning one day soon. I shall place down stones where only I decide, and I shall ponder once again the really important questions about life, about being Jewish and where my God is hiding - if hiding at all.

The cemetery in Whitefield gives me much food for thought and, rather strangely, the inspiration to ensure that life has a value. Every life - not just my own. My journey has well and truly begun and there is no stopping me now. It won't all be as desolate as this, I'm sure. But it is the journey I am compelled to take.

- My **Auntie Terri/Tilly** (Baker - formerly *Fireman*) my father's younger sister sadly died sometime after I wrote the first edition of this book and is now buried alongside uncle Harry in the plot I refer to at Philips Park Cemetery. My aunt was always very supportive of my limited literary efforts, which I took as a great compliment as she was an astute and intelligent woman who, in another era would have, like her elder brother, made a good lawyer. Like life itself, it's all down to timing.

- **Jeremy Adelman** to whom I refer in this Introduction was a year younger than me and was a genuinely lovely human being, always full of fun. I was very fond of Jeremy. He towered over me at school and, though I saw little of him after I moved to South Manchester, I remember him with real affection. He always appeared to me to be vivacious. He is not alone among my school friends who have died prematurely and who are also buried at the same cemetery. I stopped at the grave of **Anthony Schock** whom I knew well and who also attended our school, where I recall that he was deputy head boy. My heart is full of tears as I recall them both and remember happy, timeless and carefree days when we assumed that life was eternal. If they were here now, I would not hesitate to hug them both. But alas, it is far too late. A timely reminder of *carpe diem*.

- **Shtetl** is the Yiddish word given to a Jewish community or village in Eastern Europe.

- **Frum** is another Yiddish word that means pious and/or committed to strict observance of the Jewish religion

- **Yarmulke** is the skullcap, being a cap without a brim, worn by religious Jewish males at all times and by those less religious Jews at times of prayer. Otherwise known as a kippah, it is actually similar to what the Pope wears too!

CHAPTER ONE

THE JEW IN THE BEGINNING

'German puppets burnt the Jews - Jewish puppets did not choose. Puppet lovers in their bliss turn away from all of this.'

- LEONARD COHEN

I was brought up in Crumpsall in the year 1953. This would be described at the time as a 'middle class' suburb of Manchester when Cheetham Hill, just up the road from us, was moderately fashionable and quite safe, so far as I can remember. There was a large Woolworths (long defunct) as there was a William and Glyn's bank (similar) and what we then referred to as *respect*. Surrounded generally by Jewish kids, I was from an early age intrinsically aware of being Jewish and I suspect that I probably knew little else. I have only recently been back to Redford Road where we then lived and it looks a little worn - and yet curiously familiar. My roots. Nothing lavish or flashy. Very closely-knit.

In this cul-de-sac where our unremarkable little semi stood, our neighbours were almost exclusively Jewish. One was in due course to become a doctor, another a dentist and a second doctor at the corner house too. Named Weinstock, Wander and Halpern but remarkably not a Goldstein in sight. These kids were the children and grandchildren of immigrants who understandably wanted their children to be secure and to become a *'somebody'*. This was a new dawning for the occasionally merry band of wandering Jews in the post-war and post-Holocaust era. The Jewish people were now re-born and relatively free. The march of the tribe was in the ascendancy once more. Israel had gained its Independence in 1948 and lessons had hopefully been finally learned from the horrors of the Weimar Republic and its murderous protagonists. Jews were defensive but mildly optimistic. We had survived a mightily cruel onslaught, though millions had perished along the way. We had paid an extremely expensive price for being Jewish.

Professional life was symptomatic of both security and kudos, and was therefore the ultimate goal, wherever possible, for most of these aspiring Jewish parents of the 1950s. What they had been deprived of, they now wanted for their own children, perhaps vicariously. There is of course nothing uniquely Jewish about this, but it was (and probably still is) an integral part of Jewish life when I was growing up. My dad was in due course to give me certain suggestions for a career – law, politics or merchant banking - he prompted me. It seems laughable now but quite prophetic. I had absolutely no idea what a commercial bank was, but it sounded very impressive. I only knew of William and Glyn's.

I recall that I was picked up most evenings from school on a coach that transported us all to *cheder** at Heaton Park synagogue, less than a mile up the road from where we lived. This is where we were supposedly taught about Jewish things, but in fact learned next to nothing. It was there where I learned to read Hebrew much worse than atrociously, and for which we now all suffer at the *Passover** table, when I struggle to lead the service. Cheder was where we convened and where we felt imposed upon - a chore that we were obliged to endure without any actual choice.

Looking back now, I see it as an essential part of our community, and helping to promote early communal ties. I was, even as a youngster, with – *my people.* I was safe. I was protected. I was part of something, though not being entirely clear at the time what that 'something' was. The brainwashing had begun in earnest, though well beneath the surface. It was a happy childhood. I wasn't at a Jewish school, and so I was not ring-fenced, but was always aware of my religious identity. I was just Jewish.

It was a comfortable and strangely serene existence, cocooned as I was in generous layers of parental doting. This was all that I knew. The only unpleasantness I can recall was having my pants pulled down for a school medical that occurred too regularly for my liking and which played on my mind for weeks in advance. It was intrusion of the most humiliating kind, though I look back and wonder why it would have troubled me so much.

Whilst I mixed with non-Jewish children at Bowker Vale Primary School on Middleton Road, my world was one constantly punctuated by Jewish symbols. Candles were lit on Friday night; our food was kosher, both in and out of the home; Jewish festivals were generally, if not too rigorously, observed. This was my world and I knew no other – it comprised a zone with clear boundaries and well-defined values. I remained in my safe zone and as it all fitted together so neatly, I had no reason to change it, even if I could. This was my life as a youngster, when cricket was played in the cul-de-sac and the wall sufficed perfectly adequately as the wickets - chalked in with three long vertical lines against the weathered bricks. It was all pretty basic but immensely happy and uncomplicated. We rode our bicycles and dressed up for one another's parties in our best party clothes and I even vaguely remember seeing a tortoise in our garden one-day and being both nervous and fascinated. I had not seen a tortoise before and I am not certain that I have ever seen once since.

We went to Blackpool for days out where we might see Tommy Trinder or Bruce Forsyth walking along the South Pier. There was Chester Zoo too and even Lake Windermere very occasionally - such fond memories of a bygone era. These were the days when we went out *'for a run'* in the car. Now how's that for an odd concept! Petrol must have been really cheap then.

At 13, I celebrated my **bar mitzvah*** and much later on, it was presumed that I would marry a nice Jewish girl in due course. Our choice of house location was ultimately determined by the proximity of the synagogue, as it was automatically assumed that we had to be part of a Jewish community - wherever we finally settled. We soon emigrated two or three miles up the road to up-market Whitefield, as the Jews were moving onwards and upwards. We were moving to the '*country'* where the posh people hobnobbed. We would even have to learn how to speak ***proper***, though I never quite managed that one! I would be able to play cricket in a field like a professional.

Jews had traditionally settled in towns close to the railway station where they had originally alighted. They finished their long and somewhat arduous train journey, plonked down their bags where the train came to a halt and duly set up home nearby. There was no compelling reason to travel any further down the road as we were strangers in a foreign land, and we had nowhere in particular to head for. Why make yet another journey when one road was like any other road?

Gradually, as we prospered, Jewish immigrants would move further out of town and into the suburbs, away from industrial grime and smoky, dismal factories. I frequently marvel at my co-religionists of that era who moved to strange lands and yet almost miraculously learned to make a living from so little. They hardly knew the language, but they apparently used their skills and relied upon their own tenacity to progress despite their unfamiliar territory. They were innately enterprising, and their need to survive and feed a family clearly spurred them on fearlessly. I would take my hat off to them were I wearing one.

Manchester is a fine example of this. Initially, Jews settled in **Strangeways and Hightown**,* close to the centre of town, but then headed further afield to Crumpsall, Prestwich, and eventually Whitefield. Much more recently there has been a mass exodus from North to South Manchester - with its leafy suburbs and fancy restaurants. It is all a perfectly natural progression and I am confident that this pattern is duplicated throughout the Jewish world. I myself participate to this day in the Jewish demographic of the diaspora.

As I will clarify later, Jews attract Jews attract synagogues attract more Jews. It is a natural evolution and when Jews attract too many Jews, some Jews move on once again. It is a self-perpetuating drama played out in most corners of the world. We want to move on and out because, for some of us, our closely-knit community can stifle us. But then we are drawn back by the essence of who we inevitably are and what that community actually means to us. For a while we might be in denial but eventually we can soon realize that we are almost inescapably Jewish, and it can be rather difficult (sometimes impossible) to escape that simple accident of birth. It is a dichotomy – integration/assimilation – one of this next era's major issues. It can be an exceedingly delicate balance and one to which I shall be returning to consider later on my journey.

Though I did not appreciate it at the time, as a child brought up in Crumpsall, I was a member of a race and a clan as well as a religion. I felt more secure. We, the Jews, apparently the so-called *chosen* ones, were the survivors of the pogroms, the death camps and virulent anti-Semitism on the streets of many European cities. We were the *Yids*, the outsiders, the *Shylocks*, the *Fagans*, the usurers, the moneylenders, the unwelcome immigrants. We were the unwelcome guests at the party. In short, I think one can safely say that - not everyone liked us. We had been cast out. For some, we had even apparently been responsible by proxy for the crucifixion of Jesus Christ. Anti-Semitism has history and gravitas too. It is ingrained in the fabric of society and can be jolly hard to scrape off society's windscreen.

It is far too easy to be labelled the victim - a label I desperately wish to avoid. But we have certainly pulled the so-called short straw with quite alarming regularity.

Yet, we are also the survivors - the descendants of foreigners, who had generally worked hard to integrate up to a point by establishing businesses and earning our own living, and normally with minimum state help. Against all odds, we had indeed survived and even occasionally impressed some of the indigenous population with the cohesion of our thriving and vibrant community. Though often of limited formal education, many Jews demonstrated remarkable business acumen, but which then perversely caused yet further resentment from our hungry critics.

We became renowned for being self-sufficient, hardworking and charitable especially towards those who were disadvantaged within our own community. Immigrants, often ill equipped, with limited command of the English language, we frequently excelled in business in quite a notable way. Though, as I have said, we often gained begrudging admiration, there were many who remained fearful of the encroaching Jewish influence that I may refer to as the 'Rothschild factor'. We were a risk, not always welcome, and to many we presented a positive threat. We were 'taking over,' 'controlling, ' and even 'invidious.' Our insignificant minority (still numerically very small indeed) was punching above our weight once more, and re-kindling age-old jealousies that were lurking not far beneath the surface. The Jews were at risk of being too apparent.

We were the Christ killers, and yet we are rather incongruously emulated and admired too. Every celebrity on the pages of OK magazine and elsewhere appears anxious nowadays to claim some vague Jewish ancestry, however tenuous. They must presumably wish to be ***chosen*** too, but for what? I have no idea.

In fact it sometimes occurs to me that the world has a love-hate relationship with Jews. I think occasionally that I do too - though for entirely different reasons. I refer to myself on occasions as the 'Jewish Apologist' explaining away many of our less attractive traits. Madonna, meanwhile, turns to ***Kabbalah**** (Jewish mysticism) whilst Kirk Douglas, especially in more recent years, returns to his precious Jewish birth-right and prized writer, Howard Jacobson (who, as it happens, went to my primary and secondary schools) has a real penchant for Jewish characterisation in many of his novels. We just can't get away from it all. Maybe it's just the tribal instinct in all of us, but Jews are just Jews. We may not want to be part of who we are, but to escape altogether is not that easy.

As I saunter off to the cemetery, so too do many other Jews who have once tried so hard to escape the harsh constraints of the Jewish ghetto. For me, it is a poignant return to my roots. These are my roots that are firmly entrenched. Part and parcel of the person I believe I am.

Growing up as I did in the 1950s post-war era, it was relatively uneventful and peaceful. The war was well over and in the distant annals of history. The anti-Semitic Oswald Moseley was certainly marching somewhere in England but thankfully not in my back yard. I had missed the war by only a few years, and these were the solid, unsophisticated, pre-i-pod, pre-internet and pre-Oasis days defined by a degree of civility and understandable relief. I saw no rationing in my day. We dressed up when we travelled into central Manchester and swear words were well off bounds. These were what all adults imagine were their good 'old days.' Memory can distort as well as it can retell.

In these times of which I speak, we were unaware of violence on the streets or anyone smoking anything significantly dubious - other than an occasional Capstan or Woodbine. We probably thought marijuana was a place in Cuba. That's not to suggest that this was the entire picture of course as undoubtedly there has always been crime and disorder of some description in every epoch. Paedophiles, we now know only too painfully, are not a unique creation of the 21st century and have been around since time immemorial.

After a horrific war, as when I leave the cemetery, those who survived were just grateful to be alive. I am sure I can recall hearing air raid sirens going off at Agecroft just a few miles up the road from where we lived, whilst I was at Higher Lane primary school in Whitefield. They were a timely reminder of danger and the terrible price of belligerence.

This was the period of conspicuous light blue three wheelers transporting the disabled and real community '*bobbies*' actually on the beat. It was before the days of that most irritating concept of all - *political correctness.* It was a different world - partly better and yet partly worse. We have moved forward and yet we have moved a good few steps back. What did we know of 'Public Inquiries' in those days?

In the times that I am talking of, I believed in God – well, because I just did. It was presumed rather than discussed. There was without doubt one God, a listening God, a compassionate God, an omnipresent God, which all seemed to make perfectly good sense to a young lad like me. The truth is that I knew nothing else. To be candid, I am not even certain that I gave it that much thought, though I admit that my memory is not infallible. I was conditioned to believe and so I did. It was assumed and so I assumed. I was taught to listen and I was compliant. I was just a kid. Maybe I was gullible or perhaps I was just not thinking. Whichever it was, I never failed in those days to be a 'sort of believer.' He was my God. I had little to complain about.

Our God was just part of our family and He had done me no wrong. We were all happy enough and it seemed to work well. My God was Bette Midler's God, somewhere in the clouds and looking down paternally on us all from a distance. It felt better to believe, and it was much safer to accept my own parents' explanations and assurances. It was a world of no options that filled a void and helped to make life comfortable. God was there - somewhere and everywhere. White beard or not, he was on our side.

We lit small coloured candles at ***Chanukah****, just as we sat in the ***sukkah**** at ***Sukkot.**** There was always a Jewish festival to look forward to. I can see the attraction of believing in and celebrating these rituals, which provide a set order to life itself. I suppose as a child it made me uneasy to ever contemplate that it might not be so and that no one was looking after us after all. Others might call it brainwashing but whatever it was, it worked for me, at least for the time being. I did occasionally wonder to myself who might have created God and I did lose some sleep over this particular conundrum because I suspected even then that I would never find the answer. I was right. Hey presto - I never did.

I did not fully understand the concept of *faith* but willingly went along with it, particularly when the elders of the synagogue fussed over me as if I were rabbinical material in the making. I was described as 'cute', because I was so small for my age. I can remember basking in the glory of the constant attention that I received. I was on the brink of being annoyingly precocious. I held a ***havdalah**** candle in my hand, pretending that I knew what it really represented and what I was actually doing. I mouthed the words in Hebrew, though I frankly had no idea what they meant. It was Jewish custom, and that was justification enough – this was tradition. This familiarity did not breed contempt.

Some fifty years later and only now, as you can see, have I become obsessively preoccupied with the significance of my religious identity. Only much later on do I fully appreciate what I do not know. Only latterly do I know how utterly confused I am bound to be when I have no idea from where I came (other than from the womb), why I am here, for how long I am staying and, finally, where I am bound for next - should there indeed be a life beyond this one. I currently have a plethora of questions, but very few answers as I embark upon my journey of self-discovery.

Only at this relatively advanced stage of my life can I truly understand why others cling onto a religious belief, if only to avoid the inevitable alternative – ***chaos***. I fumble around in search of answers to these troubling questions and reflect upon the fact that I appear to be the proverbial ***Wandering Jew -*** still wandering in my own vast, endless wilderness searching for my personal oasis and wondering about the true meaning of life but, far too often, in a total daze and in my own state of bewilderment.

I possess an almost unbreakable pride in my Jewish identity, and yet I am unclear what that this identity really is. Being Jewish without knowing what being 'Jewish' really means. Being - without knowing; knowing - without understanding. It is a disconcerting dilemma for me and arguably for others too.

Knowing ***what*** I am but not knowing ***who*** I am. Knowing I am here, but not knowing for what great purpose - if any. I am searching in something of a panic for the answers that have always eluded me, and for the questions that I have sub-consciously avoided asking. Whilst undoubtedly Jewish, I am nevertheless an outsider who can at times be both uncomfortable with my Englishness but equally ill at ease with my Jewishness. I am on the outside looking in - an English Jew and a Jewish Englishman; I am both and yet neither. I am on the periphery, sometimes choosing to be reclusive and forced out of necessity to be isolated. I cling on to my Jewishness for grim death, desperate not to let go entirely.

I was In Manchester Crown Court, defending a soon to be convicted serial murderer from Rochdale in Greater Manchester when the devastating news broke of the intentionally evil demolition of the New York Twin Towers, and thousands of its former occupants. At first, I assumed that, like most others, I was hearing about a tragic plane crash. When the true extent of these events gradually became clear, I was unable to comprehend the enormity of those pulsating and innocent bodies plunging to their inevitable death from the smoke-filled sky. It was wholly shocking to behold, even on a distant television screen. It was horrendous and distressing. It was the moment in my life when the world had gone truly bonkers. Life as we knew it ended and assumed a different face. Evil was staring right at us. We were all in a state of genuine shock and unconditional disbelief. Its scale was unspeakable and their motives inexplicable.

It was, I believe, a CNN reporter who said at the time that the world would change from that moment on. This proved to be an understatement as, over the course of time, it has come to pass and the world is a very different place indeed. Any element of logic appeared to have been entirely ignored as the perpetrators created their own version of mass destruction and hysteria on an indiscriminate and heartless scale. Life was absolutely devalued in a matter of seconds as the planes were pointed at their multi-level targets. The glass windows shattered loudly and brashly as the towers helplessly caved in, as if in slow motion and like a pack of playing cards blown away in the grip of a tornado. Rubble covered the emergency services as they frantically beckoned the terrified crowds away from the crime scene amid the huge grey, swirling fog. The NY skyline was transformed beyond recognition and, whilst the ground was laid temporarily bare with rubble and a huge gaping hole where once there had been imposing towers, families were decimated for eternity. There remained a huge area of empty land and many more empty lives ripped apart and savaged in the name of someone else's vision of God. Buildings – values - lives - all blown apart with absolute and indiscriminate impunity. This was a day of absolute darkness when the light of sanity was turned off and humanity was desecrated as evil took command.

11th September 2001 was indeed the day that transformed the world and the specific day when I was forced to think harder than ever before about the true meaning of life itself, and the many religious followers of all religions and none - some in search of paradise and others following their own scriptures. I readily accept that there are fundamentalists and bigots of all persuasions, but the unprecedented mayhem that day which had been apparently justified entirely on religious grounds was more than enough to make me question my own religious identity and evaluate the risk of every kind of fundamentalism. I started to consider the extent to which I had been conditioned too.

It was terrifying to behold and was a declaration of war without tanks. Their weapons of mass destruction were planes full of innocent passengers, destined to be slaughtered whilst the soldier was a deranged fanatic hell-bent on the other person's destruction, as well as their own. They had a cause. That made it even more troubling. Random deaths sacrificed for an apparently religious cause.

I remember many years ago, some American Jews in Hebron, who were presumably fundamentalists of another kind, but with their own deranged agenda, who were allegedly responsible for the murder of at least one Arab. I seem to remember a Jewish *frummer* called* Baruch, who justified his actions in the name of God too. I hung my head in shame. Chosen, I asked? Chosen to take life away? Not for the first time, I recognized the potential risk of any person believing that he has the only answer, adamant that his way is the *only* way, and thus entitling him to monopolize the kingdom of God. I see these danger signs regardless of which religious group is involved - including my own.

Most alarmingly, these events of 9/11 were not the actions of vandals perpetrating gratuitous violence, but the deeds of those who acted in accordance with what they perceived as their strict religious beliefs and with the purpose of securing their personal passport to Paradise. I gather that they fervently believed that they were acting with God's authority and blessing - and in His name. They were proud men - determined, very determined but in truth with no genuine connection to true Islam. Terrifyingly difficult to comprehend.

The demolition of two huge and imposing towers and the merciless destruction of thousands of lives were so utterly vile and vicious in their intensity and scale that it was bound to make me totally re-evaluate *who* and indeed *what* I am, and what the Jewish faith, or indeed any faith, should actually stand for.

This catastrophic event was life changing as well as life-destroying. In my own lifetime, no single event has had a more profound and lasting impact upon me than 9/11 in defining who I am, and to what extent my personal Jewish identity really matters to me.

This has prompted me to consider whether religion might be a 'cloak' behind which we can all hide, if only to enable us to justify our particular agenda. Do I myself stand guilty? Is the line between faith and bigotry distinct at all? Is God a plea in mitigation to a charge of murder? Did I witness, on my television screen on that particular September day, acts of passion, belief and misconceived conviction? Or did I observe human nature gone entirely berserk? Did I witness conviction or insanity? Did I watch valour or cowardice? Did I see devotion or the devil?

As a direct consequence of the tragic events of 9/11, I ask myself right here and now whether religion has the power to create evil just as easily as it can nurture and promote goodness. To put it rather crudely - **can religion be a justification for murder?**

I question whether my passion about being Jewish is capable of justifying my own perversity, be it in the Middle East or elsewhere. Am I in danger, in my own small way, of becoming a fundamentalist as well? Do I too hide behind an unproven concept, euphemistically referred to as a *religion,* in order to justify my own actions to myself? Do I fill the vacuum with material emanating from innovative scholars rather than any proven or plausible logic? It may be that I also just 'make things fit' because it suits me to do so.

My head is spinning and I am in a state of flux. I am the proverbial *Wandering Jew* - wandering around in a stupor as I contemplate that New York void and the long-term implications for future generations of these acts of gross and vicious terrorism. I witnessed the desecration of life itself that day - as we all did. And it was beyond shocking. Horrific well beyond anything I myself had ever seen.

And so it is against the background of those defenceless bodies catapulting themselves to their tragic and needless death that I go in desperate search of my inner Jewishness.

It is not, after all, just in the cemetery where I feel so fiercely Jewish, reeling off familiar names etched onto solid stones, but also when I wander in the English countryside. I feel Jewish in towns as I do in the country. There is something inside me that might be real or might be fake. I talk about Jewish things. I have Jewish mannerisms. I am drawn to a religion that I do not understand and to a God to whom I have never spoken. I have an undeniable passion for all things Jewish and yet I frequently feel so remote from true Judaism.

I hope my own obsession is not comparable to the fervour of the terrorist who plants the bomb, who steers the airplane into the tower and who packs himself with dynamite in order to blow himself up as well as random, innocent bystanders otherwise going about their daily business. But I worry profoundly that being passionate about one's religion is arguably a double-edged sword. I am concerned that religious fervour is the first rung on the ladder to terrorism. I am also concerned that I may interpret being ***chosen*** as being ***superior.*** I build a ghetto where only Jews congregate. I can sometimes blindly and automatically justify Israel's acts of arguable aggression. I stand at the Wailing Wall, and feel moved to the point of shedding more tears. I am at risk of being a part of this divisive process, of not building bridges but rather erecting perimeter walls.

It is, therefore, in these circumstances that I am going in search of my true Jewish identity. Although my journey begins in Phillips Park on a crisp and silent September day, the path I take will be determined by the Jew I am, in order that I may finally establish what being Jewish really means to me, and what life itself may mean as well.

This is the ultimate journey of a Jew - as I am ***coming home***. My journey has just begun and this book's true story will sometimes be painful, frequently liberating, yet always illuminating for me as it maps out my journey back home. This is a journey not just of self-awareness but also of self-discovery - warts and all.

I have never embarked upon this journey before if only because I did not know. I did not know because I did not question. I did not question because it made me feel uncomfortable to do so. I felt more secure in my own safety area, where God's existence was never questioned. Without Him, I might be doomed. With Him, I was special and under his protective wing. Without Him, I stood alone and vulnerable.

This is my moment for finally confronting those many uneasy truths and even arguably a few demons. I have been to the cemetery where life ends but where my journey starts. I know that it is here that my journey in search of my true Jewish identity must commence with absolute transparency - and so it will.

I am *the Wandering Jew* coming back home. I embark on my travels with an open mind, though I am acutely aware that my heart is beating fast, my soul laid bare, and I carry my own baggage.

I am open to all persuasion as I tentatively go in search of my own personal Jewish identity. And so the search of this particular Wandering Jew to discover who he really is now begins in earnest with no way back. This is the road I have chosen and I ask you to join me. Side by side.

- **Cheder** is a school for Jewish children in which Hebrew and religious knowledge are (allegedly) taught.

- **Passover,** otherwise known as Pesach, is a Jewish festival in springtime commemorating the liberation of the Israelites from Egyptian slavery.

- **Bar Mitzvah,** literally meaning 'son of commandment', is in reality the elevation of a thirteen-year-old boy to manhood. This is a celebration when he reads from the Torah, and there is often a gathering of family and friends to mark the special moment of transition.

- **Strangeways / Hightown** are areas of North Manchester close to the city centre where Jewish immigrants settled with their families, and where they set up businesses, as my own paternal grandfather did, trading as Fireman Stores on Julia Street (our name was subsequently changed to 'Firman.')

- **Kabbalah** is the ancient Jewish tradition of mystical interpretation of the bible. Most Jews like me have no knowledge of what it really means, though it appears to have gained recent notoriety by virtue of a curious celebrity following.

- **Chanukah** is a festival that recalls the rededication of the Holy Temple celebrated by the lighting of coloured candles on each of the eight days. It is one of the more light-hearted Jewish festivals (forgive the pun.)

- **Sukkah / Sukkot** are both the festival and the building associated with the festival. Sukkot translated means 'Festival of Booths' but is generally known as the Feast of Tabernacles. It follows the serious New Year (Rosh Hashanah) and the fast day of Yom Kippur. This is much lighter and is marked by many distinct traditions. It is a festival associated with eating, which is done in the hut, otherwise known as the Sukkah. The Sukkah is a temporary hut constructed for this festival, and should sit beneath the open sky. Draped with hanging fruit, the roof is open and there is a direct line to the skies. There are, I am informed, many rules that govern its construction but it appears that the most crucial rule concerns the open roof.

- **Havdalah** is a prayer that marks the end of the Sabbath and Jewish holidays at nightfall. The ritual involves lighting a special candle with several wicks, the blessing of a cup of wine, and smelling sweet spices – signifying the sweetness of the Sabbath.

- **Frummer,** as one might guess, is the person who is *frum* or observant of the Jewish religion. When I use the term in this book, it is never intended to be a derogatory term, though can sometimes be interpreted as such.

CHAPTER TWO

THE 'YOU DON'T *have* TO BE JEWISH' JEW

"If we were to choose just one, there would be no way to deny that Judaism is the most important intellectual development in human history"

- **DAVID GALERNTER (Yale University professor)**

About six years ago, we were driving along Piccadilly in London close to Hyde Park when I spotted a diminutive figure chatting away in an obviously animated way to his friend - shuffling and stuttering along the footpath. Immediately, I abruptly and rather inanely brought our car to a screeching, unscripted halt, parked up in a side road, nearby and hurriedly rushed over spontaneously to the smaller one of the two, nearly tripping over myself in my haste to reach him, lest he make a speedy escape.

'*Jackie*' – I shrieked like an absolute fool.

He looked up towards me rather bemused, possibly irritated and understandably baffled. He tried in vain to place me, though we had never met before. He did not know me from Adam. Why should he?

'*Jackie*' - I spluttered again, rather insistently.

'*You are my hero*' - I exclaimed like a bumbling buffoon. I waited for his acknowledgement. None came. There was a silent smile.

He grimaced patronizingly and patiently, as if he might have been through this many times before. I did my best to wrap my arms around his expansive shoulders and bulging frame. I managed to crease his smart blue cashmere overcoat with my impromptu hug. I crunched him like a walnut, as if he were a close family member from whom I had been recently parted for an extended period of time. I seemed to tower over him like a giant, as I appeared to possess him and his short body. The renowned Jewish comedian from NY - Jackie Mason - was not a tall man.

We are both Jewish with common ancestry, with a sense of mutual belonging and an unspoken pride in our Jewish identity. I am the Anglophile and he the American and both of us are thoroughly and undeniably Jewish. We are, I am advised, both descendants of Moses. We are the proverbial, Wandering Jews whom I have been speaking about.

After my hearty and far too exuberant and intrusive embrace, I clutch my newly-acquired autograph as if it were a Picasso, as we both march off in our opposite directions destined probably never to meet one another ever again in this particular lifetime. But who knows?

I smile to myself as if I had climbed Everest - having so painlessly accomplished my objective of meeting the king of Jewish comedy and touching his coat and giving him an uninvited embrace - even having a treasured one-way conversation with myself. He didn't crack a single joke for me - but he did eventually smile.

Jackie Mason had, in his much younger days, trained to be a rabbi, but his true vocation was to amuse Jewish and non-Jewish audiences at Carnegie Hall and other renowned concert halls with his comic genius, and inspired timing. He has long delighted in parodying his fellow Jews, highlighting a range of idiosyncrasies of which (I can vouch for this) there are sometimes far too many. He has spent his time observing his co-religionists at all times of day and night, and reminding them of their funnier side.

Whilst we Jews generally deplore anti-Jewish remarks made by outsiders, we rarely resent another Jew poking fun at ourselves. Jackie has long been a pithy observer. Just before the intermission in one of his shows, he accurately anticipates the inevitable conversation among the predominantly Jewish audience during the break:

> *'If there are 65 rows in the theatre with 25 people in each row, 3 tiers and each ticket costing $50, he is earning much more than any rabbi I know. No wonder he became a comedian.'*

Jewish people, both by nature and nurture, tend to be both commercial and competitive. This once-observant comedian plays on those and many other common Jewish characteristics. Rather than observing the Jewish religion, he now observes Jews. The comedian's observations are at worst exaggerated but generally pretty reliable. They parody us and, on a personal level, we recognize the person he is describing because it is either someone we know or, in fact, ourselves. He babbles on and on, whilst the audience chuckle and roar at themselves. Jews really do love laughing at Jews.

Mason and I meet like old '*buddies*' bang in the middle of the pavement, primarily because we are both Jewish and there is an assumed affinity. We are not closely related and yet we are brothers; we have not met before, nor will we probably ever meet again, but we believe that we know who we both are and we have an affinity. We are from different countries and distant cities but we greet one another fraternally. We are Jews from different worlds - but we are Jews nevertheless. We are part of a boy's brigade called *the Jews*. We are joined by a common lineage - the clan of the wanderer. The Jewish people.

Jackie allows me, albeit with a little trepidation, to hug him and I do so enthusiastically. We have an inherent understanding borne out of a shared ancestry and a well-documented journey. We have much in common, but we probably believe that our shared territory is more than may actually be the case. We feel safe in each other's grasp. I think he did – he certainly didn't scream out loud.

Many years earlier, whilst I was once again in London, after watching the stage show 'Fiddler on the Roof' for the umpteenth time, I went to the stage door at Her Majesty's theatre on Haymarket in order to meet Alfie Bass (of 'Bootsie and Snudge' fame) who had been playing the lead role of the amiable and traditional milkman Tevye. Though not nearly as formidable as Topol, who had definitely made this remarkable role his own, Bass was nevertheless acting out this cherished character with genuine conviction. He was small in stature, totally lovable and possessing a great big Jewish heart - worn proudly on his torn Judaic sleeve. He not only *played* the part, but he positively *felt* the part. He was charming and engaging.

As he carefully descended the battered stone staircase to greet me, still wearing his Ukrainian boots from the show, I saw the vision of Tevye - plucked from the shtetl and approaching me warily. As he came closer, I was rather mystically catapulted into a bygone world. Like a baby in arms, I began to cry hysterically and uncontrollably. I was in my early 20s at the time but I sobbed like a distraught infant cruelly separated from his mother much against his will. I was well aware that I was crying for those Jews who had perished at the hands of their aggressors, a scene demonstrably portrayed with deep emotion in the show I had just watched yet again. I had listened to those mesmerizing tunes – 'Tradition' 'Sunrise Sunset' 'To Life To Life, Lechayim', every song and every lyric piercing right through my receptive heart.

Little Alfie Bass swept me into his arms as if I were a baby desperately in need of consolation. I was, for these precious moments, spontaneously reliving the pogroms - that shtetl – Anatevka - and the widespread suffering of the Jewish people. These were special, unique moments together. Unscripted. Unplanned.

We were two Jews. I, an anonymous youngster in the audience – he - the practised stage and television actor. We were nevertheless both brothers in arms as we embraced one another on the theatre's cold, well-worn steps, being drawn together by our shared ancestry.

Having never met before, we clutch one another as if we are members of the same family. We are two Jews meeting for the very first time, joined not in matrimony but in the recollection of mutual suffering and the bond of our religious and cultural identity. It was emotional at the time, and brings a tear to my eye even now as I recall the genteel Alfie Bass willingly and lovingly clutching me as I sobbed. It was a memorable moment or two for me. I did not need to explain to him why I was upset because he knew and he fully understood. We knew too well the suffering our people had endured throughout all parts of Europe and beyond.

I once met the renowned Israeli spoon bender, Uri Geller in a Nottingham television studio in other rather curious circumstances. I was appearing on a moderately inane discussion programme, as was Geller. The show in question was in three segments and I was appearing in the second part, he in the third. It was either John Stapleton or Nicky Campbell presenting this particular one.

As I finished my brief and inconsequential appearance on air, I was dawdling along the Carlton TV corridor when I suddenly became aware of a door to my left opening cautiously and a thin wily figure standing authoritatively at the partially ajar door, his hand firmly on the handle. His tall frame towered over me. I looked over to my left, and it was Geller himself. He discretely if not somewhat oddly beckoned me into his Green Room. I was both quizzical and flattered by this impromptu invitation and I duly spent the next twenty or so minutes in the convivial company of his family, whilst they watched intently their cherished family member's appearance on the programme, one of many I am certain that he made at the time.

When Geller returned, an appreciative and predominantly female crowd was pleading with him to demonstrate his spoon bending magic, and in frantic pursuit. He soon obliged, only then to graciously slip me the seriously bent spoon with which I proudly went home, signed by the man himself. I have it on my desk in front of me right now and reflect from time to time on this curious sequence of events. It was a peculiar set of circumstances that even to this day I have never been able to account for with any absolute certainty, though I can confirm that I didn't observe any psychic phenomena at play.

The two of us had never met before. At the time, he - a spoon bender/illusionist/magician. I - a lawyer. Both Jews. I assumed at the time that it was not by chance that I had been summoned into his Green room, but because he had realized that I was Jewish. There was an unspoken bond between us and we were part of our worldwide Jewish family. We met for the first time that night, and we were both aware that we were part of a clan, a community and a fraternity. We have a common history. Brothers.

I spoke with Geller's wife, his son and his brother in law whilst Geller himself was making his brief appearance on screen, as if we had known one another for years. I had never met any of them before and I did not even know their names before we met that night in a television studio some distance from home.

These three seemingly unrelated encounters were not bound to happen, but took on an additional meaning for me personally because all four of us were Jewish. There was a connection between us - an understanding and a meeting of minds. This is either real or perceived, though I cannot be certain which. I refrain from suggesting that I am a member of a privileged secret society that enables all doors to open for me, as it's just not like that. I have no monopoly on any Green Room and rest assured that there are many Jews who would avoid me like the plague, preferring to shut the door in my face rather than inviting me in. But there can be a certain affinity between us.

We are individuals, but we are a collection; we are strangers, but we are related; we are distant, and yet we are neighbours. Whether it is a stronger bond than between members of the Moslem faith, Weightwatchers or the Boy Scouts - I cannot say, but there is definitely a connection, inextricably binding us together by virtue of the journey that other fellow Jews have taken in the past. We Jews can have a homing instinct, just like pigeons, and there is an element of synergy as is presumably the case with any ethnic group. We have much in common with one another and yet strangely enough we have nothing.

I never really knew Mason, Bass or Geller personally but I think that I know what makes them tick - because we are all Jewish. I might be right or I might just be clinging on to a desire to be part of something that I cannot define. It is what I shall refer to as tribalism because, to some extent, this is what it is. To put it more crudely, it might be little more than supporting the same football team.

Though I was to meet Geller again, this time in Manchester, I never met Bass or Jackie Mason again. I was very sad to hear of the death of Alfie Bass back in 1987, aged only 71. Despite it being so long ago, my meeting with him remains a cherished memory for me on my Jewish journey.

And so this is an integral element of my personal search – what is my Jewish identity and what do I actually have in common with all these other Jews?

What does 'being Jewish' truly mean to me?

As I drive along Bury New Road in an area of North Manchester heavily populated by some of the more religious Jews in our area, I pass the frum Jewish girls striding along the footpath purposefully, and in their orderly droves. Clad in their customary long black skirts, almost trailing the pavement, they cause neither me nor anyone else to my knowledge any conceivable offence. They chatter politely to one another as people do, and they generally mind their own business. They look older than their years - serious, modest, even a little greyish, but I am clear that they don't mean to cause trouble.

They travel in each other's company, but certainly not in gangs. They don't drink or swear to the best of my knowledge, though they often distance themselves from their Christian neighbours. They march towards home or to their synagogue in straight lines and in something akin to military style.

These demure young ladies do not wear designer clothes, skirts with slits or torn denim jeans, but do look content enough, though definitely modest by any modern day standards. They look so poker faced - as if childhood might have inadvertently passed them by. Their dutiful mothers wear their **sheitels***, whilst their fathers and brothers adorn over-sized black trilbies often trimmed with rings of fur. They all appear to be in a hurry to get to their next religious service of which there seem to be so many at all times of day and night. They can often be seen late at night walking these streets in what, we are informed, is an era of increasing anti-Semitism. They are resilient - if not entirely oblivious. To me, even as a Jew, they live in a totally different world to mine. They reside in their own enclave. They believe and I would like to.

I spy the sons in their own expansive black hats, their creased white shirts and unshaven faces, who usually look about 40 years old but who are barely half that age. There is a real splash of black and white. Colour is out for them in all seasons. In the same way as we have no flowers at the graveside, so these girls don't go for any splashes of colour either. It is modesty personified. The men in black and white. The women in black and white. It's like a black and white movie, but with no gangsters. A plethora of grey, drawn, uniform faces.

These Jews live their lives a million miles away from mine, fairly isolated from Englishmen, and immersed in the daily practice of Judaism, the religion of my birth and theirs. These co-religionists of mine tend to keep themselves to themselves and make no real effort to mix (as I have already said) with people of other faiths - a fact that I do find immensely troubling.

The conflict between integration and assimilation may always have been an issue, but it has never been a more urgent one than in this era of international turmoil and terrorism, a subject to which I shall again return later.

I am bemused by these Jewish men's black and white uniforms, and the frum girls' pasty grey faces, and am bound to consider what if anything I really have in common with these religious Jews. They appear settled, innocent and devout, and yet I cannot help but worry for them. I see a chasm between us - like the Red sea parting for Moses, a gulf that I find difficult to bridge - though I do try.

I am sure that *I* should read the Torah, but I am equally convinced that ***they*** should dip into the Sunday Times. I need to learn to be more understanding and tolerant of difference, but even I discover that it's not that easy. They can be different from me. Very different.

I marvel at their simplicity, but I am also slightly unnerved by an undercurrent of some serious brainwashing that I automatically associate with their devotion to isolationism.

On the other hand, I have seen on the television news the frum Jews, with their ***tsitsit*****,** (shawls with tassels on all four corners worn on the outside of their clothing and often hanging down) tending, without the slightest hesitation or obligation, to the seriously injured in Israel following any form of terrorist atrocity. I am humbled by their dutiful deeds of true Godliness as they pick up body parts and treasure any possible remnant of God's creation - regardless of creed. They have a God who has not yet found me, and they appear to have answers - for which I am still frantically searching. On these dreadful occasions, they are loyal servants of God and I cannot help but feel a great surge of pride - reassured by their loyalty to their fellow man. If this is religion, then it cannot be altogether bad, I think to myself, as I rather pathetically and helplessly look on. I witness their frequent acts of unbridled compassion and willingly admire their faithful devotion - hoping it serves us all well.

But at the other extreme, I hear distressing tales of drugs and wife abuse among some of the ultra-orthodox, which allegations, though uncorroborated, are bound to perturb me. These rumours may be spread by those who wish to cause mischief, but I do worry for those who might be suffering in silence. I am concerned for the victim under pressure to conform and yet too ashamed to speak out. They may have faith, but not strength to weather all storms. There is talk of similar pressure being brought to bear upon some Moslem women to wear the burka, and so this may signify a common theme of male supremacy, though in truth I really do not know. Whether it is scaremongering or the truth is a matter of pure conjecture, but we need to keep an eye on the situation. I fear that the risk with being very frum is that some may feel caged in and occasionally they may wish to escape and explore the other world from which they are barred. I just wonder. Again, the truth is - I do not know.

I ask myself whether what I witness in Prestwich or in Stamford Hill is a form of '***fundamentalism in a furry hat***.' These fellow Jews do not contemplate packing their rucksacks with dynamite, but they may abuse their wives for failing to toe their strict and rigid party line. I find myself being frustrated that even those who allegedly have God on their side can appear to fall well short. There again, I remind myself that they are fallible too and my expectation places the bar far too high.

I am curiously uneasy when I travel along Singleton Road and nearby Leicester Road, entering an unfamiliar world where the Warsaw Ghetto has bizarrely moved location to suburban Salford, but on this occasion by our own choice. I am fidgety because we are so conspicuous and yet we are so remote. These Jews are part of who I am and yet they are a million miles apart. A part maybe, but part of another world as well. *Are we - a part or - apart?* – I just can't be sure.

Whilst I have no desire to be intolerant of anyone else's religious beliefs, I can feel uncomfortable where the ultra-orthodox proliferate and from which place even I can feel easily excluded. I am ashamed to admit it, but this is how I privately and secretly feel inside my confused head. It appears that I am challenged or even intimidated by difference – albeit within my own community. I am looking in on an enclave that refuses to move on with the times, preferring to remain in a bygone era with which I am almost entirely unfamiliar.

I catch sight of a sign on the billboard, emblazoned with the triumphal message – '*the Moshiach** is coming' and I wonder whether I am losing the plot altogether. I ask myself who the *Messiah* truly is and what is taking him so darn long to march down my particular street. This is just what I can't comprehend, no more so than Jesus being the Son of God. These are concepts that do not come easy to me. There again, I haven't read much of either the Torah or the Old and New Testaments in any depth and, perhaps until I have, I should really keep my trap firmly shut. For the time being, I am finding it very difficult to grasp these concepts – the bible, its stories and the fundamental principles upon which each of our religions is based. I liked them as fairy stories but as history books, there is still some more reading required.

I am at my most hesitant when I hear of those who are so totally convinced of the Messiah's pre-destined arrival. I cannot myself visualise hell or angels or God Himself. I wonder at times like this whether religion is any different from superstition or any more valid than dealing out the tarot cards. As I get older I seem to understand less and less. I am less dogmatic, less certain, less willing to be brainwashed and more inclined to accept that I just don't know.

Might it be that all of this '*believing stuff*' is no more than a symptom of a desperate need for a true purpose? Like a Kit-Kat or a Mars bar, it merely fills a gap. **Take a break - find religion**. It eases the pain by believing there may be someone out there looking after us all. Despite my recurring doubts, I have always felt a sense of duty to remain silent and to imagine that that our redemption is imminent and that souls are truly winging their way at this precise moment to a better world. God willing.

I try to be *spiritual* – without knowing exactly what I mean precisely by that word. Whilst I recognize the benefit of having faith, I cannot merely make it fit because it suits me to do so, any more than I can accept that the Pope is God on earth merely because others tell me so. And so, despite having a longing to find faith, I have not discovered the answers I am desperately searching for.

These religious Jews are Jews - my brothers and my sisters - but I do not dare to suggest that I know who they really are. We live in the same city and we are of the same religion, but we are otherwise unrelated. We live in different hemispheres, though we have a shared heritage. The current routes we take are materially dissimilar and we inhabit our own distinctive bubbles. They live and breathe their Jewishness, whilst I tend to dip in and out.

I occasionally wonder whether these very Orthodox Jews, clad in their frockcoats and elaborate headgear, actually recognize me or dare to even accept me as part of their flock. In a sense, we are so different that we are mutually exclusive for most of the time. I ask myself to what extent I am tolerant of them. We are part of one another's lives, and yet we rarely if ever talk to one another. I do not understand them, and I suspect that they have no immediate desire to understand me. We create barriers, though they do me no harm. These are the divisions that exist within the boundaries of Jewish observance and should really be broken down, but remain firmly entrenched.

Sometimes we are brothers, but at other times we are nothing more than distant cousins. We are separated by the same religion that binds us together, seeing life very differently and spending our time occupying totally different spaces. We park in different parking lots. We speak a different language. We pray to the same God - but with different convictions, frequency and intensity. *Is their God, my God?* I shall have to return to this awkward question at another time, and only once my journey is more advanced.

These religious Jews go to synagogues in *shtiebels**. They dress in their special and distinctive clothing. They can often speak with a distinctive intonation and an undulating tone, and they study the *Torah*, day and night. And they pray at least three times a day – morning, afternoon and evening. In their cosseted world, I am under the impression that they regard me as an outsider, if not a heathen. I am Jewish – but not Jewish enough. Meanwhile, to adopt Jackie Mason's own phrase, they are Jewish too but just ***too Jewish***. We stand beside one another when we are threatened, but at other times there is an enormous gap between us. There is no conflict between these sombre Jews and me, but there is not much understanding either and our respective lives are poles apart. Our bible and our priceless heritage are shared, but our daily lives diverge. What bring us together are the rituals that we share with our Jewish identity – the Jews, once more and forever - the Wandering Jews. But we wander along different paths and in different directions.

The fact appears to be that these Jews of whom I talk merely want life not to change, and for the simple existence once enjoyed by the Jews in Eastern Europe to be preserved for eternity. They prefer modesty to modernity - faith to lawlessness. I see nothing intrinsically wrong in this approach other than there is a risk of this attitude and lifestyle being divisive in the context of a troubled and turbulent world. Once again I return to one of my recurring themes - the dividing line between assimilation and integration. They might argue, as many do, that when the German Jews began to assimilate in Europe that was precisely the time when Hitler was able to rise to power. And they may well be right on that point.

I must also recognize the work of the **Lubavitch*** movement, a particular branch of orthodox Judaism worldwide whose tentacles extend to the most remote parts of the world and who are also dressed in similarly austere attire, though appear to adopt a refreshingly inclusive attitude towards their fellow Jews, breaking down many of the barriers to which I have just alluded. '*Gay*' for example is a word in their vocabulary and, whilst not quite ***condoning*** the practice of homosexuality as such, they are, as I understand it, at least ***accepting***. The Lubavitchers are marginally more liberal and certainly more modern in their attitudes than many other traditionally ***Hasidic**** Jews. They dress in the past but are willing to communicate with the present. They have gained a wide and loyal following throughout the world as they unashamedly celebrate their Jewishness by inviting all Jews, religious or not, to join them. They dance, they drink and they celebrate the festivals in an exuberant way, and they extend their hand, their time and pockets to the needy. They do really good work whilst cherishing their Jewish identity. They regard the future of the Jewish people as paramount, a sentiment with which I can empathise entirely.

As with any other religion, Judaism is open to endless interpretations. There are many shades of opinion and a multitude of disputes between those who interpret the word of God in their own particular way. I am just like every one of them, a Jew - a proud Jew. I am proud of my membership of this oppressed ethnic group that has at the very least survived. And I pray from the same *siddur**, stand on the same *bimah*,* listen to the same *chazzan** leading the service, marry under the same *chuppah** and bury our departed in the same cemetery, just like the one I have described at Phillips Park. As you can recognise, we have many similarities between us, despite the fact that we also have a number of fundamental differences. One of those differences is our faith. Not even our Jewish faith as such, but our faith in God. No doubt every religion has these differences.

My faith is fragile at best, and my commitment to core beliefs wavering. In the company of those with a much more liberal approach to Judaism at the other extreme to ultra-Orthodoxy, I must regrettably admit that I can actually feel equally edgy. I feel *out of sy*nc in the unfamiliar surroundings of a Jewish Reform synagogue where women and men sit alongside one another as if in a church, and where their Jewish prayers are read in English much more frequently than in our Orthodox environment where Hebrew reigns supreme. They park their cars on the Sabbath in full view of the synagogue and its rabbi, whilst we are more discrete (and hypocritical) parking around the corner and well out of sight - if only to save the rabbi's blushes. These Reform Jews practice a modern version of the Jewish faith and challenge my Crumpsall conditioning to the core. What they say is that religion must adapt with each changing era and accommodations need to be made in order to make it all workable. They recite some of their prayers in English in order that they may actually understand what they are praying for, and to whom. On reflection, it sounds a perfectly sensible idea. And yet it's alien to me – the lad from Crumpsall. What do I know? I need to read something that I do not understand if only because that is the way that it has always been.

In the UK, Liberal Jews go even further down the line of compromise – breaking down even more barriers and taboos. I hear of female rabbis, and I see their rabbi not even wearing his yarmulke, and I witness a new world with which I am unfamiliar and which causes me to feel vulnerable and exposed. It is strange that I should feel so challenged by Judaism's different strains, but I do. Even when I have been to a Sephardic synagogue, though orthodox, its tunes are different and I am not quite at home.

These different interpretations of the Jewish faith need not actually cause a rift between us at all - but they can do. Though claiming to be liberal and tolerant, I have been tormented by my own bigotry. There are many shades of Jewish belief and, just like different branches of Christianity high and low, we Jews are often in internal conflict between one group and another. We all have our own version of our own Jewish faith, and even I can fall into the trap of believing that only my way is the right way. All of us are at risk of turning into fundamentalists - unable to embrace difference even within the boundaries of our own religion. It is quite shameful when one element of a religious group will not even share a platform with the other. This happens and when it does it reflects poorly on all of us.

In making this admission, I am even at this early stage of my journey realising that I need to embrace difference *within*, as well as *beyond*, my own religion. I must work hard on this. Like a terrorist who straps a bomb-filled rucksack to his back, willing to sacrifice not only innocent lives but his own life as well, I am at risk of believing that my way is the only way forward and that somehow only I have the true path - that other Jews have it all wrong. Too religious, not religious enough, and though I am pretending not to, I sit in judgment on others as if I am entitled to do so. As I journey along, I need to start learning a little more about tolerance.

Incongruously whilst in New York I hurriedly head for the East Side where immigrant Jews once resided in their own part of town, and then on to the Jewish Museum near Central Park. I jump on a congested ferry across the Hudson River, anxious to see Ellis Island where Jews and other immigrants once arrived as their portal from Eastern Europe and maybe elsewhere. At Ellis Island, I look excitedly for family names on plaques and in books, but draw a resounding blank. I stand beside framed photos of bearded black-coated, stooping Jews armed with their battered valises, sadness in their eyes, and pathos etched on their wrinkled faces. These people are an integral part of who I am – wanderers lost, separated, oppressed and vulnerable. But with a last hope in their eyes too.

On a much lighter note, whilst still in NY, we frantically search for the Jewish delis and eventually discover one called Ben's located close to Times Square, where the salt beef is heaped high on rye bread and is, by all Jewish benchmarks, culinary ecstasy. The huge, curly new green cucumbers are oozing garlic and accompanied by some exceedingly spicy tomatoes. The kosher meat is divine. This is the ultimate Jewish experience that in Yiddish we call *fressing* and translated means more 'devouring,' than merely 'eating.' This too is a vital part of what being Jewish is truly about. We eat our food with great relish (forgive the pun) and a salt beef sandwich epitomizes what being Jewish is all about. This is part of my Jewish identity as well.

As a Jew, I don't feel threatened in NY. I am in the company of other Jews and I am aware that America, particularly New York, willingly, and for at least most of the time, opened its doors to Jews in trouble, Jews on the move, refugee Jews and those Jews who were wandering from one country to another at that time. They came, often via Ellis Island, to a brand new world and fresh opportunities in the Big Apple. This is where their cases were plonked down, and this is where they made a new life for themselves, as I have described elsewhere. This is where many Jews were bound for, though in fact they ended up in sunny Manchester, as my grandma did - according to her Russian passport which reads: 'Bound for America.' She never made it there. The ship stopped somewhere unfamiliar, and she found herself in Northern England.

Whilst we are cruising in the Mediterranean, we dutifully hurry along to the obligatory Friday night Sabbath service, where we congregate with fellow Jews nodding politely to one another. Speaking different languages, many of us will rarely go to synagogue when we return home, but here some of us get *busy*. We sing along to the same familiar songs that we sing at home, and some of us pretend to pray once more in a language we do not understand. It's illusory, but great fun - being part of this distinctive tribe. We assume that we know one another and that we have much in common. We smile, we munch on a chunk of bread, we sip the **Kiddush*** wine and, whilst effusively shaking hands with one another, we wish mere strangers a good Shabbos, after which we rather hurriedly saunter off to dinner in the main dining room. This is undoubtedly tribal through and through. It is a club of which I am a life member. This is where, on a Friday night in the middle of the ocean, I belong right now with my people. We are part of an extended family just like the Jewish boys, religious or not, at my school. We were the Jews; we remain Jews. Rich Jews, poor Jews, dirty Jews – we were, and are forever, the Jews. ***Chosen for what?*** God only knows.

And wherever I travel in the world, especially far from home, I search out the local synagogue as a matter of apparent urgency. I know from what other Jewish travellers tell me that I am not alone. I do not go to pray but to feel at home with something that is an integral part of me. I climb up a steep hill in Dubrovnik to visit one. I walk along the side streets of Versailles to look up at another, as I do in Istanbul. I seek out the shule in Turin and an ancient one in Rhodes. I look up towards the sky - just in case He is there in the distance looking out for us after all. Yet again, I am returning home to my Jewish roots. These synagogues all have a similar appearance and all pay homage to a God whom I am looking for. They celebrate longevity and they epitomise continuity for me and that alone can be a source of real comfort.

I have returned. I have peeled away my veneer and I have discovered a layer of Jewishness that is at my core. I have an insatiable, instinctive yearning for synagogues whenever I travel abroad and yet, when I am at home, I sheepishly and rather speedily drive along Bury New Road where the local synagogues proliferate. My attitude serves only to highlight my inner turmoil. These are good and harmless people, but they are odd to me. There is distance between us, as they return to their patch and me to mine. My response is confused. Sometimes I go in search of Jewish places of worship, whilst at other times I hurry by almost ashamedly. Allegedly proud to be Jewish, I seem intent upon ignoring the ultra-Orthodox, whilst I search out those same religious Jews when far away from home, as if to remind myself who I am or who I think I ought to be.

I am tormented as I search for my identity and what '***being Jewish'*** really means to me. It appears as though I have a cultural attachment to my Jewish faith, and yet a much more fragile religious belief. I am a thinker but only seemingly in the foggy mist that I have created for myself. I seem to practise my Judaism, only from behind a lace curtain.

It is therefore abundantly clear that I am one exceedingly confused Jew. If not, why would I ever have to search for the nature of my own Jewish identity? I still like to dress in a suit on the Sabbath, and I love the Sabbath candles on a Friday night. I find the notion of retaining a rest day each week most appealing, and I adore many of the tunes that we sing on ***Kol Nidre****. I stand at ***Neilah**** like a well-trained soldier. Even I too get ***busy***, as if I know what it's all about once again. I am in my own battalion and I become a ***somebody*** when people know me and nod at me and even dare to shake my hand. This is the Jewish tribe, the Jewish people – seemingly at prayer. In reality meeting up as fellow Jews, the Wandering Jews.

An erstwhile friend in Liverpool sends me a text out of he blue – '***gut voch'*** - he says - and I am visibly touched by his conventional Yiddish greeting that when translated simply means nothing more than '***have a good week.***' It is as if I am in receipt of a coded message. I am drawn in mysterious ways to a religion that beats inside my chest, but for reasons that I cannot precisely comprehend. It is a religion I am close to, but which I can easily find intimidating and irrelevant. It is part of me and yet, on a certain level, it seems archaic and redundant.

I question it. I overlook it. I disregard it. And yet most of all, I absolutely love it. I have never read the '***Midrash'***, the '***Torah'*** or the '***Rambam,'*** (the seats of Jewish learning) but I have the audacity to seriously evaluate my own beliefs, whilst questioning the faith of the ultra-Orthodox. I am a fraud, too lazy to learn what I do not know, and with the boldness, if not barefaced audacity, to make a judgment of others I am not qualified to make. I write a book about my Jewish religion, but I fail to properly investigate its many facets and intricacies.

What I have, in fact, described is what I referred to earlier as my own love-hate relationship with Jews. I feel everything and yet –just sometimes - I feel nothing. I am proud, yet I am ashamed. I feel an important part, and yet I am in total isolation - as I revert back yet again to being the eternal *Wandering Jew*. I have much in common. I have nothing in common. I think it's rich. I think it's irrelevant. I knew everything. I know nothing now. This is the starting point for my embarkation on my Jewish journey of discovery.

When I first discover Israel, all these contradictions come to the boil in the ethnic cauldron referred to as the *Holy Land*. It is to Israel that I travel next in order to lean about other important aspects of my Jewish identity. I need to discover my connection with this faraway land, apparently promised to the Jewish people by the Lord Himself and whose Temple wall reverberates to the sound of Jews of all religious persuasions visiting this predominant symbol of Jewish survival and where we share our own innermost thoughts in prayer. This is the country that truly celebrates the Wandering Jew and brings together all shades of religious belief and none.

It is *'Eretz Yisroel'* (the Land of Israel) to where we Jews believe we can escape *if* ever the next pogrom is unleashed upon us. It is hardly surprising that for most Jews it is a country with which we have a profoundly emotional attachment and I am no different. In the aftermath of the Nazi onslaught, it was the refuge for the dispossessed Jews from all corners of the world.

To discover every aspect of my own Jewish identity, I now travel to Israel, the Promised Land, promised to the people of whom I am chosen to be one.

I continue my personal search for my own Jewish identity by wandering to the home of my people in Israel, accepting that it will always be difficult for me to be wholly dispassionate about justifying its existence and true purpose.

I am hopeful that this particular Wandering Jew will discover not just a land but answers to some of the most fundamental questions that have troubled him for so many years. It is, after all, my ultimate bolthole. It is the Promised Land.

And so this is where I must head for next.

- **SHEITELS** is the Yiddish word for a wig or half-wig worn by some Orthodox Jewish married women, in order to conform with the requirement of Jewish law to cover their hair as a symbol of modesty.

- **TSITSIT** is a blue and white-corded garment (prayer shawl) with tassels on the four corners worn by Orthodox Jews.

- **MOSHIACH** is the Messiah in Judaism. The belief in the eventual coming of the Moshiach is a fundamental part of traditional Judaism.

- **SHTIEBEL** is yet another Yiddish word meaning 'little house' or 'little room,' and is a place for communal prayer, and is a less formal place than a synagogue.

- **LUBAVITCH/LUBAVITCHER** is a philosophy and a movement, being Orthodox and part of Hasidic Judaism. The Lubavitcher is the person who is part of Lubavitch, otherwise known as Chabad.

- **HASIDIC** is a branch of Orthodox Judaism that promotes spirituality, emanating from Eastern Europe.

- **SIDDUR** is the prayer book for synagogue services.

- **BIMAH** is the podium in the middle of the synagogue from which the cantor sings, and from which the Torah is read.

- **CHAZZAN** is the cantor and who leads the services in the synagogue. He is generally associated with a melodic singing voice.

- **CHUPPAH** (this is not a cuppa, as you can't drink one of these) is the canopy under which a Jewish couple stand during their wedding ceremony.

- **KIDDUSH** is a ceremony and blessing over wine on the Sabbath or a holy day. Literally, it means 'sanctification.'

- **KOL NIDRE** and **NEILAH** are two prayers, the first is annulling vows made before God sung on the evening of Yom Kippur, the Day of Atonement, whilst Neilah is, in fact, the closing service of Yom Kippur and in translation means 'closing of the gates' – the last chance saloon before God decides our fate. Scary!

CHAPTER THREE

THE JEW IN ISRAEL

'Every Jew, no matter how insignificant, is engaged in some decisive and immediate pursuit of a goal. It is the most perpetual people of the earth.'

- JOHANN WOLFGANG VON GOETHE German Dramatist & Poet

Israel's Independence in 1948 followed on from the Balfour Declaration that finally provided for and recognised a home and refuge for the Jewish people. This followed persecution and repeated displacement at the behest of the Nazis in the Second World War's horrendous and extensively documented Holocaust. Though denied by a few, for most decent people this sustained programme of systematic extermination of the Jews is an undeniable historical fact and a serious and unprecedented stain on humanity. Despite what the so-called historian David Irving has repeatedly claimed, most fair-minded people appear to acknowledge begrudgingly or otherwise the historical fact of the annihilation of more than six million Jews, as Hitler assiduously pursued his declared ***Final Solution***. To understand me, and who I truly am, I am unable to ignore these dreadful events of monumental enormity and evil. They have contributed, in no small measure, to the character and dimensions of my Jewishness. They go to the root of who I am.

Born in the 50s, I knew only of an independent State of Israel, though regrettably I have never fully understood its history. I know that the British were in that area prior to Independence, but I cannot be certain as to who had the prior legal right to land in the region and therefore hesitate before ever sitting in judgment. I gather that the Palestinians were offered and refused partition, but I have never verified this in any thorough detail. I prefer my *'middle ground'* and the *'measured approach.'* Clearly for those who believe that Israel was God's gift to the Jews, their interpretation of events will be greatly influenced by that premise. I am not at present in that particular camp.

Whilst not every Israeli is Jewish and nor every Jew a Zionist, the relationship between the Jewish diaspora and the very concept of Israel is doubtless one crucial aspect of defining my own Jewish identity. I admit that I have an innate sense of allegiance to Israel, as it is to whatever extent a part of who I am. If anti-Semitism on a grand scale erupted across the United Kingdom tomorrow, I could escape to a place of safety in Israel, where I would be made most welcome and where as best as possible I would be protected.

I also marvel at the awe-inspiring achievements of the Israelis in building a solid democracy since Independence. Though often abrupt, the Israelis have demonstrated remarkable resilience, gritty determination and hawkish resolve. They have created a technologically advanced democracy, where the arts and academia are flourishing. This is all the more commendable because of its insignificant size, being a slither of land, surrounded on all borders by those intent upon its destruction. Rather than solving anti-Semitism, as former Zionist pioneer Theodor Herzl once predicted, Israel can inadvertently actually fuel the anti-Semitic rhetoric. But when Jews are under threat, we search out other Jews if only to establish a defiant wall of resistance. We are, in addition to whatever else we may be, a fraternity as I have already said with a well-established sense of allegiance to the land of Israel.

The suggestion that the establishment of Israel would eradicate anti-Semitism altogether is not well founded at all. There is at the present time much evidence of anti-Jewish sentiment across the globe and when Israel either defends or attacks its neighbours in Lebanon or elsewhere, justifiably or not, it is even more prevalent. There are many who are happy to equate Jews with Israel, and Israel with aggression. Israel is no longer the eternal underdog and can no longer rely upon the public's sympathy vote that at one time it appeared to have permanently secured. Nowadays Israel is often portrayed as the aggressor, the protagonist and the over-influential land grabber.

There can often be a peculiar relationship between Jews and Israel as certainly applies to me. I have an almost unflinching sense of loyalty founded selfishly upon my own survival, as well as the survival of the Jewish people. Yet on another level I feel strangely uncomfortable. In fact, on the subject of Israel, I appear to be as ambivalent as ever. Like my religion itself, Israel too creates a number of conflicting emotions.

I first visited Israel when I was about 11 years of age. It was Passover when I went with my family on a cruise sailing from Marseilles via Athens and Las Palmas and ultimately bound for the port of Haifa in northern Israel. I felt very privileged at the time, and even now so many years later I can still recall a massive surge of excitement at the prospect of visiting Israel for the first time. This was the era when travelling anywhere abroad was significant in itself, but the land of Israel for Jewish people was bound to be particularly special. There was mystery, pride, nervousness and a real burst of euphoria.

There was hope in the air that day. Yet more than 50 years later and Haifa is under constant threat from Hamas's rockets whilst the residents of this tiny country remain at war with their adjacent Arab enemies. Whatever the reasons for this endless animosity, it is sheer madness that it prevails. No doubt being naive, I remain hopeful of a solution with no more blood spilt on both sides. Following the collapse of Mubarak in Egypt, the demise of Libya's tyrant Gaddafi and Bashar al-Assad's Syria in tatters, the future is less certain in the entire Middle East than ever before - explosive and precarious in the extreme. But I remain, as I always do, the idealist, the ultimate optimist. I live in eternal ***Hope***.

When I reflect upon the fact that I was born just a few years after Israel's Independence, it makes my head ache, both in anger and in despair, in so far as a smouldering war can still be on going in the 21st century. Peace is discussed fleetingly at the UN or elsewhere and then just bypassed with all those concerned accustomed to fighting over land and waging war and treating this cycle of violence as just inevitable. It is self-perpetuating and seemingly with no realistic end in sight. I just won't accept that.

The S.S. Jerusalem, the ship upon which we were sailing to Israel, was operated by the Israeli Zim line - a company that, so far as I am aware, still thrives today. The vessel was full of Jewish people celebrating

Passover. Rabbi Felix Carlebach, who was the Rabbi of South Manchester synagogue in Didsbury at that time, led a service that resembled a huge, extended family gathering. In Israel, they have just one *Seder**, whilst in England we sit down to two because there is reputedly a lower level of spirituality in the diaspora. It was quite an occasion. This learned and loquacious rabbi who died many years ago was larger than life itself. He was cultured and articulate, of German extraction, possessing a profound love of opera and of all things Jewish and musical. All the children at the time including me stood in a wiggerly line at the front of the dining room reciting the *ma nishtana**, a prayer generally sung by the youngest member of the household if old enough and translated as the *four questions* which are addressed to the father. Whilst one of the prayers at Passover talks of *'next year in Jerusalem'* – we didn't have to wait that long. For us, it would be just a couple more days at sea, and we would be arriving at exactly that spot or thereabouts.

This trip was especially memorable for me for another totally unrelated reason. As we passed through the notorious and often merciless Bay of Biscay on our return to Marseilles, the ship started to roll so vigorously that almost everyone fell instantaneously sick. The ship was battling against the waves that were belting against its hull. I know that ships at the time didn't have stabilizers as they do nowadays and were bound to be more vulnerable to these stormy conditions, but this sea was positively vicious. Even Eve Boswell, the cabaret at the time, had to succumb to sickness, leaving an audience of just one, my father Jack, who quite remarkably never suffered from either sickness or headaches at any time during his lifetime. He was literally the one single person out of several hundred passengers on board that ship still sitting in that once-congested cabaret lounge – Jack Firman, my dad, the only soldier still standing on that fateful night on the SS Jerusalem. He now had nothing more to listen to, other than the fierce winds and the ferocious ocean when the vocalist and her musicians were finally forced to pack up their instruments in their cases and surrender to the seriously tempestuous elements that night. And even my defiant father finally gave up if only for the fact that he had no company left - returning to our cabin where the rest of us had all felt deathly for ages. We were by this time praying to reach France so that we could disembark at Marseilles to escape those relentless torrents. Give us land – we prayed desperately. We became frum in these extreme circumstances.

But what I thankfully and most vividly remember of this voyage is our emotional and momentous arrival at the port of Haifa. Israel was then in its embryonic stage and our anticipation was palpable. The dream of a Jewish homeland and the prospect of a safe haven for a displaced people were being lived out, whilst the *kibbutz** seemed to genuinely represent true brotherhood in ignoring the usual incentive of private profit and endless greed. This really did appear to be the land of dreams where God's promise had been fulfilled in our own lifetime. It was tearful. It was exhilarating. It was momentous.

At this time, crime was negligible in Israel as it was seemingly the land of hope, youthful aspirations, religious fulfilment and a home for all those who had been so recently and tragically persecuted. It was a vivacious, pulsating country and Jews en bloc flocked to Israel, if only to bask in its glory with some considerable pride. It represented a haven where Jews could hopefully live in safety and harmony within its own borders. For those more religious than me, the handing back of Israel was seen as a pure miracle. We were **returning home.** Jews who had conventionally cowered were now ready to boldly and defiantly defend themselves, destined to build a respected army and a Middle-Eastern democracy of considerable repute. Jews were ready to redefine who we were and who we now are. Those who were creating a country from the desert were real pioneers and remain a source of inspiration to me even to this day. Deserts became oases, rubble became towns, and shacks became houses. It was a remarkable achievement and transformation.

As we approached Israel, the cruise band played the Hebrew song '**Hevenu Shalom Aleichem,**' a traditional and evocative Hebrew song, the meaning of which in English is appropriately '**we brought peace upon you**.' For seventy subsequent, belligerent years that much heralded peace aspiration has eluded this particular country with each side inevitably blaming the other for the on-going and costly conflict. On this particular day as we arrived at the port, there was only hope and optimism in the sea breeze temporarily blowing away the horrors of the Second World War. Arriving in the Promised Land, we were each *very* Jewish this day as people returning to the land that we had read about in the bible stories of our childhoods. It was awesome and an unforgettable and priceless experience. Exceedingly special.

Passengers were bristling with uncontrollable delight as the land of Israel was within our grasp and in our sight. Though young at the time, I was acutely aware of the joy that permeated the ship with lines of passengers thronging the varnished, wind beaten, wooden decks on their voyage of discovery. Many of them I suspect discovered themselves in the bargain. It was impossible not to be moved by it all. Israel the '*land of our people'* was in the distance and moving closer and closer, and now distinctly in view. We edged nearer, until that moment came when finally the anchor was lowered and en masse we triumphantly marched down the gangway onto that sacred land - like heroes. The victors.

In our Passover prayers, as I have previously mentioned, Jews pray that we will spend *next year in Jerusalem,* and now the reality is that we are actually here, in the land of Israel. Many of those on board openly shed tears on what was our first and memorable trip to the Jewish homeland. It was indeed as if we were *returning home*.

We were thousands of miles from England, the place of our birth, but our affinity to Israel was undeniable. Though thoroughly English, as Jews we were aware that Israel was the land which God had allegedly promised to the Jewish people and where we would forever be offered a safe sanctuary. We had all become momentarily religious, relying rather conveniently upon God's promise. It suited us at this precise time to believe in God's will, as we could then witness our very own miracle. As often is the case, many of us *'made it fit.'*

These were the early days, well before the war of 1967, the Yom Kippur War, the war with Lebanon, with Hezbollah and with Hamas, before Begin, Meir, Sadat, Netanyahu, Dayan, Rabin and all the others who have helped to define and redefine the shape of the Middle East. Little did we appreciate what the future had in store for this Jewish retreat, and the unchartered waters that were to be negotiated beyond the Mediterranean Sea. We were dreamers then, just dreamers, with no notion of what lay ahead. We were just living the dream. We did not hear the sound of gunshot.

The altercations, the boulders, the guns, the tanks, the injuries and the needless and tragic deaths that were soon to separate the Jew and the Arab were to make the Bay of Biscay look comparatively calm and almost welcoming. A sad and tragic path lay ahead that was never contemplated by us on our initial visit to Israel. We were euphoric as we *returned home*. Religious or not, there was something that made our hearts instantly and spontaneously flutter as if like a butterfly winging its way across the olive groves in the Judean hills. I believe that each one of us was proud to be Jewish as that ship docked in Haifa at that time when we were regarding this land as our biblical heritage. It was an unforgettable journey as emotions ran high and dreams were fulfilled. This was Zion and we stepped out onto its land heads held high and in triumph.

My father had been involved for several years with a charity called CBF (Central British Fund) that was subsequently re-named World Jewish Relief. Their purpose was, and as far as I am aware remains, to provide financial and other help and support to Jews in need worldwide, however remote or disbursed they may be. Some years ago I had the enormous privilege of going on a mission with WJR to Odessa in the

Ukraine on the edge of the Black sea. This charity often seeks out Jews in some far off villages many miles away from the city, providing food and sustenance for the needy. They do what Jews are renowned for – looking after our own, whatever our religious affiliations may be. It was an exceptionally moving trip and made me particularly proud once again of my dad who had throughout his life worked tirelessly for this as well as many other charities as well. He had been the treasurer at Hillel House in Manchester, a charity that provides housing and support for Jewish university students. He did work for Abbeyfield (a charity for the elderly of all denominations), and also did more charity work for our shule. His charitable record puts me to shame. He even found time to be involved in local politics for the Labour Party in Whitefield alongside the late Joel Barnett who subsequently became Chief Secretary to the Treasury and who left a legacy famously known as the '**Barnett Formula.**' He was a lovely man who always dressed immaculately.

I vividly recall going on a coach to a distant village whilst on my WJR trip where we met an elderly Jewish lady living alone in a high rise flat and in abject poverty. We went with a kosher food parcel for which she was enormously grateful. This was a truly commendable example of **Community.** I think their work is incredible and the notion and reality of 'community' is at the very core of what being Jewish really means to me. It creates a real sense of belonging, and should ensure that we are never entirely alone. I will return to this particular thought later.

Back to Israel again. On arrival there was an announcement on the ship's loudspeaker asking for my father to come to the purser's office on board. We were concerned at first, but it soon became apparent that we were to be met by a former Mayor of Haifa who was waiting at the quayside. He had a connection with CBF and planned to take us out in his car in order to show us the whole of northern Israel in a day. Wow, what a prospect that was. As we tumbled into his car and then travelled around, it soon struck me how tiny Israel really was. Though it goes back a long time, I remember our genteel guide's neat grey beard, stooped frame and kindly face. We travelled in his battered motorcar to Acre, Tiberias, Caesarea and Safed, all cities in Northern Israel. We had been flattered when whisked away like celebrities on our special whirlwind tour, whizzing past the coaches still loading up with the other weary but wide-eyed travellers. We were getting to know this biblical land in a flash with this lovely man as our dutiful guide. He gave me my first taste of Israel and it was invigorating and enthralling. It was am amazing introduction to the Promised Land.

When I was in my 20s, I was to return to Israel, this time with a school friend, and with a rucksack perched on my curved and tired back –

supposedly destined for youth hostels. By now, some 10 years later, Israel was vastly different. There were religious and secular Jews living alongside one another who were helping to build an entirely new country out of the desert. The dream had developed into a reality and all the many Jews converging on Israel from very different backgrounds had to learn to co-exist. Israel was embroiled in a war within, as there were now fundamental differences between Jews of different religious and political affiliations from every part of the world. It was a small country and still very much in its infancy – a bubbly melting pot. Everyone with an opinion.

      I remember sauntering through Dizengoff Square, right bang in the centre of Tel Aviv, unable to find any kosher food and feeling cheated. This was not the Israel I had in mind. No kosher food? It was a joke. Things were thankfully to change over the years. I also soon realized too that I preferred the comfort of the five Star King David Hotel in Jerusalem rather than the less salubrious surroundings of the rather more basic youth hostel across the road. I couldn't afford to stay there, but I did regularly sunbathe by their pool. I was not born to hardship and old habits die-hard.

      I have re-visited Israel since on a number of occasions, though not frequently, and I have experienced mixed feelings. In Eilat, on the southern tip of Israel and facing the Red sea, I saw a fine array of luxury hotels that bear no comparison to the two small hotels – the Moriah and the Neptume - that once stood in isolation on my first trip many years earlier. The food is strictly kosher, the breakfast vast, the people frequently arrogant and curt, the landscape fascinating, the beach sometimes stony, the shops full and exciting, and the majestic land itself always pulsating and vibrant. Israel, the land of our people, the land promised to the chosen people, but by this stage a land living in the shadow of war. And so it has remained ever since – a dark shadow indeed inevitably looms large. Should God have decided to give back the land to his chosen people, he certainly makes it hard for us.

      As I have observed already, the achievements of the Israeli nation are quite remarkable, with internationally respected technicians in every field of science and medicine putting Israel at the forefront of innovation and accomplishment worldwide. In Jerusalem on another visit, all of us stand in amazement at the sight of the Via Dolorosa, Mount Scopus and the Wailing Wall. As had been the case on my first journey to Haifa, we could not help but be moved. Whether it was strictly true or not, this was the land that spoke and breathed the bible. I stood in the room of the Last Supper where it is said that Jesus sat down at the Passover table for the final time. This is the finest example of ***Continuity*** - a theme I shall return to time and time again. I think ***Continuity*** is something, as we get older, that we really value. It was as if we were returning home again and reliving those biblical stories of Abraham, Joseph, Moses and all those other renowned bible characters with which as children we had become so familiar.

Did I believe? I cannot say. ***Did it matter if I believed or not?*** Not really - it was part of my life and who I am inside - and remains so.

My relationship with Israel, as with Judaism generally, is as complex as it is confusing. Whilst I am proud and stoically loyal to a country that espouses democratic principles, I remain troubled. There are many Jews who regard it as their duty to loyally and unflinchingly support Israel and all its policies unconditionally. I understand that perfectly well. There is bound to be a deep sense of allegiance to a country willing to offer refuge to those degraded and dehumanized by their enemies. We all have not just a homing instinct but also a desire to survive. We appreciate that we Jews have the inalienable '***right of return.***' Despite this, there are many rebellious and well-meaning Jews who are willing to break rank. There are some Jews who are actually anti-Zionist, but far more who are openly critical of specific Israeli policies. There are some of the ultra-religious Jews who dare to question Israel's inalienable right to exist, almost appearing to be in cahoots with Israel's declared enemies. There are some rabbis and a number of Jewish celebrities who queue up to criticize Israeli's policies towards the Palestinians, and the settlements in particular.

I myself cannot help feeling sorry for Israel when it appears to be at its most isolated and vulnerable. I become defensive and feel a naturally intense sense of loyalty. But I also know that Israel is not always right and I try my best to take my customary measured view – the delicate balance once again. Gerald Kaufman, the once longstanding Jewish Labour MP for Ardwick in inner city Manchester, who died only recently was consistently critical of Israel, much to the annoyance of many Jews. On at least one occasion, he caused a real stir when he drew a comparison between Israel's war in Gaza and the Holocaust. Not the brightest thing to do. Some Jews responded by calling for Kaufman to be excommunicated. This was like an Islamic *fatwa*. I find such hysteria from my own community to be unwarranted, however tasteless and inappropriate his comments might have been. Allegiance to Israel cannot justify the perpetration of religious or other intolerance and I become perturbed by such over-reaction. We all need to compromise, accommodate and believe in Hope – of peace, of a solution, of an end to the bloodshed. The recurring danger is in fundamentalism – believing there is only one way, and only one side to an argument.

There is much anger, despair, bigotry and belligerence associated with the longstanding Middle East conflict. The political inferno naturally produces heated argument and intense passions on both sides. My personal concern is that Jews may use God as their shield, their justification and their crutch, just as others do and I admit to being uncomfortable with this. Israel can be right but sometimes it can be wrong too, and our own passion has sometimes to be tempered and ought not to cloud the issue. Dogma is by its nature dangerous.

At a time in the future whenever that might be, these protagonists will eventually be compelled to talk to one another, to accept the other's right to exist and learn to live alongside one another. The two state solution is frequently talked about and appears to me to be the only realistic outcome, though this is unlikely to occur in my lifetime. As to where the borders are drawn, and as to the control of Jerusalem, these are destined to always be profoundly difficult issues. Yet we must never lose **Hope**. I live in eternal **Hope**. My cup is always half full. It has to be. Many Israelis I have spoken to are not as optimistic as me, having become immersed in accusation and counter-accusation over so many years in this endless fight for land and sovereignty. I understand perfectly well that when others on your own doorstep will not even accept your existence, it makes talking about peace and long term solutions quite difficult. But talk we must even with our enemies.

In response to the incursion into Gaza, there were Jews amongst many others denouncing Israel and demonstrating against what they perceived as Israel's unwarranted aggression towards the Palestinians. There were many others who wrote in the press, openly critical of Israel for its so-called **'disproportionate'** response to the rockets fired from Gaza into Northern Israel. Foreign Secretary at the time, William Hague, used that exact word to describe Israel's response. This public dialogue – sometimes hostile towards Israel – is symptomatic of Israel's development. Jews feel that they can fearlessly speak out without denying Israel's right to exist. But the fact remains that the vast majority of Jewish people in England and in the diaspora generally feel an enormous sense of pride in what Israel has achieved in a relatively brief period, and indeed what it stands for today. It is indisputably the only true democracy in the region founded as it was after a failed attempt to annihilate the Jews off the face of the earth. Its youngsters are conscripted into the army and are obliged to defend their country and, in turn, my right to exist. It would be churlish of me not to be immensely grateful to every one of them, however vehemently I despise this ghastly, perpetual war.

That does not condone what is wrong, and nor do I deny the rights of the Palestinians. It is an instinctively emotive response. Israel is part of me and for most Jews, I am certain it is part of them too. It is part of what I was when I was a little lad landing at Haifa and what I am now so many years later - despite the passage of time.

      I have friends and family who have immigrated to Israel, and I know full well that, when other countries were wobbling, Israel stood firm as my safe house. In the wake of the Weimar Republic's determined quest for its Final Solution, it is hard for me not to regard Israel as a friend. Israel is there for me when I need her and I therefore must constantly ask myself - am I not there for her too? There is for me a sense of duty that is deeply embedded and that I have no desire to shake off - even if I ever wanted to. When young Israeli boys and girls go to war, they do so to defend my right to survive - and for me to spit in their face would be the ultimate insult.

      Yet as I have intimated, power corrupts in Israel as in every other country of the world, and there will doubtless be those who are naturally pugnacious for the wrong reasons. I have heard the Israeli prime minister, Benyamin Netanyahu, speak in the past and I have bristled at his warmongering language. I instinctively question his intransigence on the settlement issue, though I understand that it might merely be political posturing. I am desperate to see genuine compromise on both sides and I yearn for peace in the region and for it to come very soon.

      But, as with all things, I always remind myself of my favourite cliché of all – '***until I have walked in their shoes.***"

      I am one of the Jews who does not believe that the BBC is intrinsically anti-Israel. I think there is confusion between the Jew and the Zionist, and the assertion that anti-Semitism can be substituted for anti-Zionism cannot always be justified. Many Jewish people will, I know, deplore my views, and I have no wish to offend any one of them. This is an aspect of my Jewish identity I cannot ignore - fairness, justice and transparency.

      We Jews are sensitive to criticism and, bearing in mind our traumatic history, this is hardly surprising. In times gone by, when Jews cried out for help - there was a painful, ominous silence. I have watched tearful newsreels of ships bound for Palestine carrying the desperate and the displaced, and it is impossible for me not to be defensive and even resentful when I have seen boats turned back in similar circumstances elsewhere. And that is why every Jew is bound to feel for the desperate plight of the Syrian refugee and the asylum seeker escaping from their home country, living in fear and fast losing hope. The world far too readily turned its back on the homeless, humiliated Jews with horrifying insensitivity. Indeed, I have recently read of MI6 ignoring the urgent needs of those shipped out of the death camps with no home to go to. But in my darkest moments I take profound comfort from the humanity of Oskar Schindler, Raoul Wallenberg and Nicholas Winton who risked their own lives, like numerous other righteous Gentiles, to save thousands of Jews from the hands and the rifles of the Nazi soldiers. My Jewish identity dictates that I always must be there for others in similar circumstances - displaced, disenfranchised, dispossessed. The helpless in No Man's Land.

On a more recent visit to Israel in 2008, I attended a family bar mitzvah when I spent a few days there during which I had some moments to quietly reflect upon my personal relationship with Israel. I was based in Herzliya, a bustling seaside town not too far from Tel Aviv. I had time to walk alone along the beach and on the walkways. I saw bronzed, relaxed Jews, many of advanced years, merrily jogging along the beach in the early morning by which time the sun was beating down onto the beige, shiny, shimmering sand. In the numerous conversations I had with those living in Israel, they made it pretty clear that they were universally proud of their country, though not always supportive of their government. The odd taxi driver would be rather more circumspect in his praise. There was, without doubt, free speech, the hallmark of any true democracy, and all manner of opinions could be freely expressed without any fear of reprisal.

Many of my fellow guests at the bar mitzvah believed Israel could do no wrong. There was consistent hope for peace among the Jews of Israel and the diaspora, but often a genuine and deep-seated anger with their Arab foes. There was disagreement as to the terms upon which peace should ever be achieved. So far as Israel's policies are concerned, I believe that Israel does not preach hatred and that most Israelis are crying out for peace. I also deplore the fact that Hezbollah and Hamas may not even recognize Israel's right to exist and that their children might well be educated to hate – which, if that is the case - is truly dreadful. But I also listen to American Jewish fundamentalists eager to expand the settlements and I become equally downhearted and outraged. I attempt to be even-handed and as objective as I can possibly be. In the refugee camps of Gaza where the deprived and the homeless are confined and where poverty and sickness are rife, it is hardly surprising that hatred and despair proliferate. Their treatment by the Israelis, but also by their own co-religionists, can on occasions raise genuine concerns. Their incarceration is both humiliating and dehumanising, and it is understandable that it should contribute towards engendering an endless cycle of mindless violence. It is regrettable, whatever its cause, and whoever is ultimately responsible, and I hang my head in shame whenever any life is devalued. Every one of us is entitled to an 'opportunity.'

I genuinely shudder at all loss of innocent lives on both sides. Any life lost in battle is a life wasted. The incessant fighting since 1948 is tragic and has to end with eventual and brutal compromise. To me it is essentially an argument over land that will eventually end, perhaps against all predictions to the contrary just as it did in Ireland where so-called 'religious' battles raged for decades in a seemingly endless cycle of violence.

And so whilst I have a natural love and passion for Israel, for me it cannot be unconditional. Whilst in Herzliya, I considered whether the Israelis I saw running along the beach or serving in the shops really had anything in common with me other than the mere fact that we are Jewish. Were they, like the frummers striding out in cohorts along Bury New Road, from another world too? In Israel, the world is one of bronzed bodies, biblical edifices and Jews of every nationality and none. **What do I have in common with these Jews?**

There are always contradictions. We are bound by common background but not necessarily by religious beliefs. We are linked by suffering and by the Star of David on an armband, and yet culturally there appears to be an enormous gulf between us.

I walk along the road one night on my own whilst I am in Israel thinking about all this identity stuff. I spy some local families enjoying barbecues together, probably kosher - but maybe not, under the romantic beam of the soothing and stunning moonlight. I speak to a black-skinned girl from the Caribbean who guards the door at the local shopping mall, close to the reclaimed harbour where I have just been walking. I nod to her and to which she immediately responds by wishing me a *'**Shabbat Shalom,**'* a good and peaceful Sabbath - and I jolt forward to offer her my hand with ease. As I do so, we unashamedly embrace and I then for certain know that I am with my people once again and I feel safe and comfortable. There is that intangible common bond once more. This is my community where we are bound by a common heritage and a shared history. We have survived as one people. Black or white, Israeli or English, religious or not, wealthy or poor, Israeli or English, there is something that I cannot define but which, magically and rather mysteriously binds us together as one people. This young woman reminded me that we have much in common. Things divide us, but much more brings us together and can never come between us.

In Israel, the week comes to a halt on a Friday night at sunset. Religious or secular, Shabbat/the Sabbath means taking a rest, rediscovering one's identity and returning to one's community, and I love it for these reasons. To this extent at least, there is peace here. Despite the continuing hostilities, Israel remains a country of enormous opportunity, where the sun is shining most of the time and where there remains a real sense of purpose. I wonder rather perversely perhaps whether it is the constant threat of war hanging over Israel that actually provides a clearly defined objective, survival – the greatest leveller of all. The Israelis live in the shadow of war, and live their lives under a black cloud and yet, ironically, the sun shines and the country prospers in the most inspirational way.

So, however hard I try to logically assess my relationship with Israel, it is actually impossible for me to be entirely objective. Israel, though distant from my home, is an integral part of who I am. It is in my heart and is a vital aspect of my Jewish persona.

When I hear Hebrew songs sung, I am emotionally fragile. When Israel is at war, I want it to be over quickly and decisively. I fear for our survival.

In my young days, I had heard of Egypt's Abdul Nasser who forever threatened war with Israel. Nowadays Hezbollah and Hamas are, like Iran, not at all keen to even recognize Israel's right to exist. I cannot help but be protective towards my co-religionists literally fighting for our survival. But as I have stressed, my heart bleeds just the same for any Palestinian who is living in awful conditions, and for the Palestinian child deprived of a parent killed in combat. I despise this war – all wars - with a vengeance. It is appalling that this apparently never-ending dispute between these Middle Eastern people results in the loss of so many innocent lives on both sides. It has to stop. It just has to.

I can hear the wailing, the shrieking and the despair from both quarters claiming a direct line to God. I listen to the sounds of the mosque towers calling their congregants to prayer. I hear the shrill sound of the ***shofar**** the ram's horn blown at the Jewish New Year. In one hand, we hold the Koran or the Torah and in the other a grenade. This is ludicrous. In my study at home I have a print of a soldier standing side by side with a religious Jewish man and their juxtaposition is a chilling reminder of this perversity.

New York may be the 'Big Apple' but Israel is a real melting pot too - with Jews and Arabs living in a foaming cauldron, a volcano waiting impatiently to erupt again. Forever vibrant, highly technological, universally vociferous but on the precipice of conflict, it is hardly surprising that I feel a sense of loyalty to the homeland of my people. I support it as I do a member of my family with a true and loyal sense of kinship.

Though Jews did not always have a reputation for being formidable soldiers, the Israeli army soon gained universal admiration for its strength and valour. Its critics suggested that this reflected more upon its enemies' ineptitude and lack of arms than their own aptitude as fighters. Yet there was also begrudging and tacit acceptance that Israel possessed a seemingly fearless army that won miraculous wars against all odds. And so, however fair-minded I would like to be, it is impossible for me to be truly unbiased. I can be critical but only in a limited way.

And so there we have it. My relationship with Israel is similar to the relationship I have with my own Jewishness. It is full of contradictions and hypocrisy. Israel and me. We all need to survive. When our enemies threaten us, it draws us closer together regardless of our own Jewish observance. We are when under siege all Jews together. When Hitler chose us, he did not distinguish between the frum and less frum and, however assimilated, cynical or secular we were, we were all rounded up with a yellow star and a number unceremoniously stamped on our arm, much against our will.

I love Israel like a brother, a brother with faults but a brother nevertheless – a brother who will always stand shoulder to shoulder with me and defend my right as a Jew to exist. And for that I remain immensely grateful, although I still long for a lasting peace for all people in the Middle East.

I cry for every single life lost on both sides. The long-awaited peace cannot possibly come too soon.

- **SEDER** is the Jewish ritual feast that marks the beginning of the Jewish festival of Passover. In Israel, we have one Seder and elsewhere two. It is a family occasion when the child asks the father the Four Questions and the father answers.

- **MA NISHTANAH** means –Why is this night different from all other nights? This line precedes each of those four questions asked by the child at the Pesach (Passover) table.

- **KIBBUTZ** is a collective community in Israel, traditionally based upon agriculture and first established in 1909. It is based upon principles of communal ownership of property, social justice and equality, and was first established by youthful, idealistic Zionists. I believe that there are well over 200 Kibbutzim (plural!) in Israel today.

- **SHOFAR** is a ram's horn, blown as a musical instrument, akin to a bugle, at certain times of the Jewish calendar, and in particular at the Jewish New Year. It can often be a struggle to get any sort of note from it, but the fact of that struggle itself makes it more poignant.

CHAPTER FOUR

THE ARCHETYPAL JEW

"The dispersal of the Jews was both a boon and a bane, their nation was disjoined but their culture was enormously enhanced"

- **SAMUEL KARLINSKY Author**

The Jew can be frequently perceived and then described by the non-Jew as *'family-minded'*, *'good in business'*, *'careful with money'*, *'long-nosed',' clever'* and *'shrewd'*. This presumes that there is a uniform set of Jewish characteristics unique to every single Jew in the world. This is the often-misguided version of the stereotypical Jew.

It might be that these various, often derogatory, descriptions are nothing more than examples of indiscriminate and unsubstantiated prejudice. The burning question is whether this is total myth or whether we Jews are indeed 'mean', 'bright', 'entrepreneurial', 'family-orientated' and all the rest.

Can we really spot a Jewish person by our appearance or by our mannerisms and character? Are we truly a homogenous race, or a race of many different people with certain common beliefs and habits?

And so I next go in search of the so-called 'archetypal Jew' in order that I may discover other aspects of my own Jewish identity - and who I really am. The suggestion that one group of people is entirely different from the next sounds innately divisive. Whilst I myself can sometimes use the phrase '***celebrate our differences,***' I fear that these blunt and rigid distinctions may have some potentially invidious consequences. In order to establish my own Jewish identity, I desperately need to examine these various generic descriptions and test out the extent to which they stand up to closer scrutiny. For me, it is a fascinating investigation as to who we Jews really are, and to what extent we are each the same. I ask myself to what degree are we born to be different and, on the other hand, to what extent do we '***become***' different due to nurturing and environment.

When I see a fellow Jew, do I know he is Jewish and, if so, why? Does he ***look*** different, ***speak*** differently and ***behave*** differently? And if this is so, why should this be? Are we by nature moderate drinkers, or is it merely part of our cultural upbringing? Are we inherently tight-fisted? Are we really the cream of big business and, as some would have us believe, truly planning to take over the entire world? Why did Geller choose me of all the people in the studio that day? Mere chance or more than that?

I need to know who is a Jew in order that I can establish who I really am. I need to peel back the skin so that I may get to the bare bone, particularly my own. In order to define my own Jewish identity, I need to verify a few truisms about Jews. Whilst I have already referred to the lack of understanding between one Jew and another, and the undeniable divide that sometimes pertains between the religious and the secular Jew, the question is whether there are some characteristics that are common to all Jewish people. The shared ground might be the epithets applied to Jews by non - Jews. It might be genetic or it might be reactive or, on the other hand, it might be entirely illusory. I just need to know the truth about Jews as I search for my own personal Jewish identity.

Is there truly such a person as the 'archetypal Jew'?

I do not intend dwelling on statistics because they can be tedious and often have their own agendas. My starting point has to be to briefly investigate whether there is any empirical evidence substantiating the perception of the common characteristics of Jews. I ponder whether the specific term '***chosen people****'* has much to answer for, as it is a potentially troublesome and mildly embarrassing description. If a Jew wrongly interprets its' meaning, it can engender an unwarranted superiority complex, whilst the reverse is also true and those who are not ***chosen*** can easily feel excluded or even inferior. This is all bound to have some serious consequences. The fact that the term refers to a description allegedly bestowed upon a specific generic group by God can only serve to aggravate the situation further. It is hardly conducive to racial harmony for one particular religious group to have been apparently *'chosen.'*

Does the assertion that Jews are in some respects 'superior,' originate from this description *'chosen'*? The proposition that Jews are somehow ***clever*** in fact means nothing specific. The word *'clever'* means everything and yet nothing in this context. It might be intended to suggest that Jews are ***bright*** or it might infer that Jews are ***cunning***. It might otherwise imply that Jews are actually ***dishonest*** and can therefore be easily applied in both a positive and a negative way.

It is like the word ***Jew*** itself that can either be merely spoken in a non-judgmental way, or otherwise spat out with venom. The word *'Jewish'* is somehow a less judgmental word altogether than the word *'Jew'* which can have an unfortunate ring to it.

In support of the claim sometimes made that Jews are intellectually superior, there are those who refer to the Nobel Prize as a reliable and accessible yardstick. Apparently between 1901 and 2005, Jews accounted for 22% of the individual recipients worldwide of the Nobel Prize, though Jews comprised a minute proportion of the world's population. This seems to prove the proposition that Jews are somehow ***brighter***. Those same statistics can however be misleading. The Rothschild dynasty, Prime Minister Disraeli, Moses Montefiore, Karl Marx and Albert Einstein are all fine examples of exceptional Jewish talent and achievement in many fields of knowledge. There are endless such examples of attainment in literature, science, politics, the arts and business and it is commonly assumed that Jews have had a disproportionate influence on the world. This might well be so. But the Nobel Prize system has a bias towards those with socio-economic advantage, and I am reliably informed that those upon whom the prizes are bestowed generally come from professional families. It is also likely that those who ultimately win a Nobel Prize might be equally assisted by connections, networking or self-promotion, as much as by pure intellect.

Accordingly, the question arises as to whether even the Nobel Prize is a true barometer of intellectual superiority. The truth might be that it reflects more upon the background of those who eventually win the coveted Prize, and the fact that Jewish people are better connected or more influential might be responsible for this fairly extraordinary data. This demonstrates how bare statistics can be so easily misinterpreted.

I am aware that much emphasis is placed upon education by most Jewish parents, and so it is logical to assume that if a group of people strive for professional status, they will over the course of time become more educated and more intellectually refined. Whether this means that we Jews are genetically brighter I somehow doubt, as I think it is more likely to be a reflection of treating the education of children as a priority over a lengthy period of time that is the predominant factor. This is similar to Chinese immigrants to this country for example who also strive for professional status, as do many other immigrant groups who want their children to achieve a certain status within the indigenous population. It can often be the territory of the immigrant minority who are striving for status and recognition in a foreign land. Immigrants will frequently want their children to have greater opportunities than they themselves had enjoyed back home. This is analogous to religious schools – Jewish, Church of England, Moslem or otherwise – where family values and parental pressure play an integral part in maintaining and raising standards.

It seems to me an intrinsically invidious argument to suggest that Jews are intellectually superior. The corollary is equally unfortunate – namely that the non-Jew is academically inferior. But if this is in fact the case, I have to be willing to confront this harsh reality, however troubling it might be. On the one hand, I am flattered by the notion of intellectual superiority, but similarly very uncomfortable with the thought of religious elitism coupled with ethnic inferiority. I can easily see where all this talk is capable of leading, and it's not a pleasant prospect.

There are many writers who have put their own gloss on the subject of Jewish intelligence. The contemporary Jewish scholar Raphael Patai claims that there is evidence of '***Jewish pre-eminence'*** as well as intellectual superiority, whilst another Jewish author Nathanial Weyl says that intellectual pre-eminence is the inevitable consequence of ***two thousand years of selective breeding for intelligence.***

This appears to me to be indicative of the perennial distinction between nature and nurture. As long as Jewish parents value their children's education and status, more than a few will win prizes. But whether that reflects innate intellectual superiority, I somehow doubt. We would have to go back to the beginning of time to assess whether the Jew was by nature brighter than his neighbour, and I fear that is an impossible task for me to undertake in the course of this particular journey.

It is more likely that if Jewish people do excel in the professions, this reflects the desire of Jewish parents striving for their children's security and status after a long history of wandering and discrimination. This reminds me of private schools taking credit for the results of their pupils who have actually been 'cherry picked' by them at the outset, and destined to do well almost regardless of where they were educated. Their academic results will reflect more on the academic company they keep and parental expectations than just the standard of teaching.

I believe that the term, to which I have already referred, **'*chosen people,*'** is to some extent the author of much of our own misfortune. It smacks of superiority and separatism. Open to much misinterpretation, it is at best an unfortunate description and at worst - one bound to promote resentment. If God did use it, it wasn't His best choice of language to date. The term **'*chosen people'*** is almost certain to breed jealousy, and it was ultimately Hitler who turned the tables on the Jewish people by adopting a similar distinction for his own evil ends. His Aryan race was, according to the Fuhrer, the superior master race, whilst Jews, homosexuals, gypsies and those with disabilities became the blot on his perfect landscape and urgently needed to be obliterated. There has surely never been a more poignant juxtaposition of concepts borne out of a misconceived notion of superiority or exclusivity. It demonstrates the inherent danger of relying upon generalisations and stereotypes and the lethal inference that one group is superior to any other.

The ***chosen*** people we may be, but chosen by whom, why, and for what? The risk inherent in anyone believing that one group is superior to the other is obvious. Whatever Jews were ***chosen*** for, the mere fact that we were apparently 'chosen' appears to set the Jewish people apart. There is a ***division 'ab initio',*** namely from the beginning of creation. This is more about perception than reality, but nevertheless significant in so far as I believe Jews have paid a heavy price for this apparent 'choice.' It made us appear more different than we actually are.

To regard one group of people or any religious group as being chosen by God in particular is a recipe for potential disaster, and so in my opinion it has proved to be. I believe that the description ***chosen people,*** in conjunction with the accusation of Jewish responsibility for the crucifixion of Jesus Christ, have jointly played a vital part in creating antipathy towards Jews throughout the centuries. Though I shall deal with the issue of anti-Semitism later on in my journey, I do raise the question as to whether some of the rather unpleasant descriptions of Jewish people can be attributed more to this undercurrent of resentment towards Jews than as a result of applying any real logic.

There is no denying the fact that Jews have had an important influence upon the development of many societies, but I believe that this is more attributable to culture and oppression rather than to genetics and God's gift. There has been an insatiable need to survive and it was necessary to be competitive and strive for acceptance. Jews have had to be more resourceful than most other people for those reasons.

Skills in business are merely an extension of the same argument. Jews became traders and made their living by selling their wares originally in the market place, but later as rather more ambitious and prestigious shopkeepers. In the shtetls of Galicia and the Ukraine, Jews were arguably simple souls who lived for one another and in relative seclusion. They were not educated and nor were they, at this stage, businessmen. They placed their faith in '**Hashem'** (one of the several Jewish names for God). They were the ones who often lived as paupers and were isolated and probably ignored with impunity. This was just their lot and they probably knew little else. They looked after one another pretty well, being part of a true community where everyone was just about equal.

I suspect that the notion of the co-operative was not created in Rochdale, but more probably in the outskirts of Gdansk, and was likely to have been far more successful there too. These Jews appear not to have been driven by any great ambition other than trusting in the Almighty. Over the course of time, they emigrated, either by choice or by compulsion to other countries, where they hoped and believed they would be safer. Their suffering and the pogroms had become an integral part of their Jewish identity long before the emergence of the Weimar Republic. We had been excluded from all parts of the world, and so our survival became a pressing issue for obvious reasons. This remorseless oppression was bound to have a positive effect too, as it made Jews value their freedom and it made many of us natural fighters for our survival, acceptance and justice. It must also have made our dependence upon God even greater as He appeared to be the only one firmly on our side.

These Jews had learned to be tradesmen and had similarly been actively encouraged, even obliged, to become moneylenders. It was the job that no one else was willing to do and therefore often the only occupation that Jews were allowed to have. In so far as the accusation that Jewish people were 'mean,' I suspect that this probably reflects their lack of funds rather than any in-bred propensity to be 'stingy'. When you are short of money, you are forced to be careful. In all my travels, I have rarely come across a Jewish person who was in fact unduly mean or miserly, though no doubt they do exist, just as with any other group of people of whichever religion. The Jewish trade as moneylenders was destined, by its' very definition, to promote a tarnished reputation. In my experience, Jewish parents are normally generous towards their children, and many Jews are renowned for their benevolence towards religious and secular charitable causes, both Jewish and non-Jewish. Those Jews who came over from Eastern Europe or even from the Middle East were often extremely poor and their lack of funds might well have caused them to be careful out of sheer necessity, especially with the money they never had. In the case of the European Jews, It is the case that many had their money and artworks stolen by the Nazis. As a group of people, putting it bluntly, we could never feel entirely secure, and leaving something in the kitty would probably sound like a sensible idea. I think it's called – saving for a rainy day.

It seems to me that the allegation that Jews are mean by nature has more to do with anti-Semitism in the guise of Shakespeare's Shylock and Dickens' Fagan. These dreadful stereotypes are both odious and fundamentally misleading. Similar to the proposition that all Jews are wealthy, it is a statement that can be proven time and time again to be widely off the mark. I know that Jewish social services in my own city are never short of genuinely needy Jewish clients of all ages.

Turning now to physical attributes, there is no denying that I have a hooked nose, and there was not that much I could do about this other than sulk. I had no zest for cosmetic surgery and I was conditioned to believe that this nose of mine was a '***Jewish Nose.***' I am a pragmatist and I therefore accept that these are merely accidents of birth. Without wishing to be unduly modest, I suspect that I was never destined to be conspicuously pretty, even without the curved 'hooter'.

I met an old friend of mine some time ago who has an equally large nose with a similarly obvious 'hook'. I think out of politeness they call our noses '***Roman***'. This friend, who happens to be Moslem, has a nose very similar to mine. He definitely isn't Jewish but equally he has a nose of very similar size and dimension to me. I now understand that our physical attributes reflect where and how we live. In other words, the longer that Jews like me and Moslems like Hamid live in England, the more likely it will be that our children will have fair hair, blue eyes, and cute, inconspicuous noses - lucky them! These noses are merely part of who we are born to be. The so-called Jewish nose is in fact a Middle Eastern nose. My nose reflects where and how Jews have lived, rather than Jewishness itself. I can remain optimistic that my great, great, grandson, should I ever have one, will look more like an Englishman than I do, as it is far more our environment that affects these physical attributes than our religious identity. Hamid and I were from foreign extraction and we must resign ourselves to the fact that our respective noses were 'part of the package.'

It would therefore appear that, whilst there may be some element of truth to most of the epithets attaching to the Jewish people, they generally reflect the Jewish journey and our history rather than the intrinsic Jew himself. Some of the descriptions rely upon an undercurrent of anti-Semitism, whilst others are a response to the term: ***the chosen people*** or even the assertion that ***the Jews killed Christ.*** Stereotyping can be an element of indiscriminate prejudice. We can respect our differences but it can be very dangerous to exaggerate them.

I must add that I am not personally aware of any Jew wanting to take over the world, though Albert Einstein, Karl Marx, the Marx Brothers, Stephen Spielberg and others have doubtless played a disproportionate role within their respective fields of expertise, and may possibly have presented some form of peculiar threat to some who were vulnerable to challenge.

Whilst I was at school, I played cricket and, to my genuine astonishment, I was once chosen to play for the school team for which I was to keep wicket. As the leather ball was hurled towards the batsman in front of me, I held my breath and hurled myself heroically towards the projectile. Among my Jewish peers, I was the exception to the rule. There may in the history of the sport never have been a Jewish professional cricketer at county level, never mind of international standard. Similarly, there are no Jewish professional cyclists, rugby players or sprinters. Yet for some reason, there have been some great Jewish boxers, always proud to wear their Star of David on their shorts and to fight their corner. The truth is that some of these boys had learned that they **had** to fight, having learned their trade on the streets of the East End, like the late coiffure Vidal Sassoon. It was a matter of survival as is the case with the army in Israel. Football has generally been bereft of Jewish players until Israel more recently produced some notable exceptions. This once again is more to do with cultural breeding than pure genetics. We weren't great at rugby, only because we didn't play it. Snooker was not our bag because we were not spending our evenings with a pint of beer in the other hand. And so on.

The Jewish kids at my school treated sport as an unnecessary interruption, and cross-country in particular as a serious imposition. I don't think this proves that Jews can't play sport, but that Jews have not regarded playing sport as a priority or as a career choice. We were not terribly good at metalwork at school either, and I can vouch for the fact that I was positively useless at woodwork too. I think this has far more to do with conditioning than with real ability.

There are essential cultural differences borne out of immigration and excommunication. Our parents tended to be over-protective too. Our social lives were separate sometimes from the English ways. We were still learning to integrate. I was certainly never encouraged to take an active part in any sport but as I have said, I was expected to concentrate on my studies. Little did my parents appreciate that the snooker players and football players of the future were destined to earn far more than any lawyer I ever knew. They may have thought differently had they have known this at the time.

There are, I willingly accept, many similarities among Jews but there are intrinsic differences as well. There is bound to be sameness among those whose journey has been so similar. Many of our grandparents were from Eastern Europe, and those who survived the Holocaust came over to this country with little money and few possessions, having been obliged to leave their families back home. In a miraculous way, they became traders and shopkeepers and most survived. They wanted their children to have a better life and they strove hard - with this objective at the forefront of their mind. But there were also many **Sephardic** Jews, whose families came from the Middle East - Iran, Iraq, Egypt and elsewhere. Theirs would often be a vastly different upbringing as they were generally wealthier than their Eastern European counterparts. There were other **Ashkenazi** Jews from Western Europe living in Germany and elsewhere. Highly articulate and more assimilated, this was another distinct group of Jews who were educated and integrated into German society well before Hitler rose to power and became their much-lauded Chancellor in 1933.

But there is common ground. They had each known suffering at one time or another and anti-Semitism was never too far away. And as the former Chief Rabbi Jonathan Sacks has said, we have a common religion and pray before the same Wailing Wall.

As I have said, both Jew and non-Jew have a habit of generalizing when describing the archetypical Jew. Even I myself am guilty of this. There are, I recognize, cultural differences. At a Jewish wedding or bar mitzvah, the bar stocked with alcohol is unrestricted, and yet I have rarely seen anyone drinking to excess, and nor have I ever seen a fight break out at any Jewish celebration. I have joked with my non-Jewish friends that the only time we actually touched alcohol in my family was when we moved house and carried the bottles in a box to our new home. Whilst Jewish law or custom does not forbid alcohol consumption, it is not generally an essential part of our day-to-day culture. This is in the course of change, as we ourselves become more assimilated into English society. There would similarly appear to be a Jewish ethic of hard work and self-sufficiency. The crime rate among Jews is markedly low, though probably rising. It is too easy to put this down to one single aspect of Jewish life or purely our religious beliefs.

These differences are cultural, environmental and heavily reliant upon our upbringing. This has been largely defined by the concept of the ***Wandering Jew***. Sometimes insular and often defensive, we Jews are determined to learn the lessons of our history – ships turned away and former friends and acquaintances quietly turning the other cheek. It is easy to see, even in these relatively enlightened times, why we continue to feel so vulnerable, having been customarily treated so badly numerous times before. It also appears that the scourge of anti-Semitism is on the warpath once more. The statistics are not encouraging at all right now and tragically the lessons of history are not being heeded. Lessons will be learned, they say - but when? I read of anti-Semitism in Germany, in France, in Eastern Europe as well as on my home patch in England too. It is a constant worry. There are many willing and able to whip up hatred, be it against the Jew or the Moslem or both. There is a Le Pen in every era and in every zone and they are longer necessarily on the periphery. They are marching to the same tune founded on scaremongering.

I consider how these various descriptions actually apply to me. Big nose? As readily admitted already, I am guilty. My father had a large nose that I inherited and, as I have accepted, this causes me no particular grief or alarm.

As to intellect, I got through my law studies only by being a '***slogger***.' My memory can be truly hopeless and, whilst I went to a Grammar school and even in the top stream, my A levels and subsequent University results were unexceptional. I fail the Einstein test miserably, though I definitely fought hard to get the grades and always worked assiduously as I still do to this day.

Most of my Jewish friends were driven by raw ambition with considerable emphasis being placed upon professional achievement and accomplishment. Children from Jewish homes were almost inevitably driven to strive for more. There was a keen sense of direction, as many were destined for professional life and the apparent security that this offered. This attitude had much more to do with insecurity than innate intelligence. We were encouraged to be competitive, if only for the fact that it was perceived as necessary for survival's sake.

The accusation that Jews are notoriously mean is not, as I have already said, borne out by my own personal lifetime experience. Religious

Jews are obliged to donate a percentage of their earnings to charity and often do. The reputation we have is in my opinion without any true foundation.

Both Jews and non-Jews are convinced that Jews are just different, and to some extent they are right. Many Jews drink less, stick together more, work harder, articulate well, aspire to more and have protruding noses. Some Jews are mean, whilst most of us are not. Some are extremely ambitious, and some are not. Some Jews are wealthy, but many aren't.

The similarities between Jews result from a common history as an itinerant people – repressed and frequently banished. As a result, we Jews can be over-defensive, resentful, defiant and proud. It is often discrimination itself that has drawn we Jews together. This is not pure religion - but pure culture. This is the odd distinction that inspires me to seek out a synagogue in a far away place in order that I can feel close to my own people. It is curious that, as an English Jew born and bred in Manchester, I should have this peculiar affinity to my Jewish brethren in other countries. As I have admitted, I pass by the frum Jews in Broughton Park, another area in Manchester where a large number of religious Jews reside, and yet search out my religious Jews in distant lands. This all takes some explaining.

The notion of the archetypal Jew is often overplayed and misconceived, as well as being potentially discriminatory. There is nevertheless a common history, predominantly emanating from Eastern Europe where Jews were obliged to protect one another from pogroms. In so far as Jews are different, we are a product of our culture and our religion. We have been oppressed and displaced time and time again. This is who we are and this is who I definitely am. I am not a victim – but I am the product of the victimisation of others.

My conclusion is that we should embrace difference but not exaggerate the differences between us. There are many types of Jewish people, and our similarities are sometimes far less significant than we all might believe. As well as difference, there is humanity - common to all.

In my search for my Jewish identity, I have chosen to devote my next chapter to the history of anti-Semitism and its substantial impact upon me. We are in an era in which we are told that anti-Semitism is on the rise in many parts of the world as a result of which Jews are immigrating to Israel from France, the UK and elsewhere. As always, I intend to take a measured approach towards this sensitive subject in order to establish its effect upon moulding my Jewish identity. I tend to believe that anti-Semitism has tragically never gone entirely away - but merely ebbs and flows – though we shall now see as my journey takes me through some muddy waters.

CHAPTER FIVE

THE DIRTY JEW

"Our duty is to incite Jihad against America, Israel and their Allies. We believe that the affairs of many of those are moving in the right direction and have the ability to move widely. We pray to God to grant them victory and revenge on the Jews and Americans"

- OSAMA BIN LADEN 1998

I pleaded with my father not to do it, but he was as always absolutely determined and he refused to listen to me and my feeble protestations for one single, solitary second. He was adamant - as was his custom. For Jack Firman, there was an important principle at stake. There was to be no compromise. Jews had to stand up for themselves – no more appeasement. This was the voice of experience speaking to me loud and clear.

I recall sheepishly striding up to the Headmaster's study with its well worn, stark and imposing oak door on a crisp winter's day. It was as if we were on a mission and indeed we were. This was a showdown and for Firman senior, Master of the Household, and he who ought to be obeyed, there was a point he *had* to make, and make it right now. The headmaster *was* going to listen, and there *was* no question about it. When my dad made up his mind, nothing was going to shake his resolve or stand in his way. No ifs, no buts, no feeble excuses.

The venue for this rather theatrical event was none other than Stand Grammar School in Whitefield, just up the road from the cemetery where my father was destined to be buried many years later, and where you and I visited earlier. I am aged twelve at the time and small for my age. In the second year Form 2L – the *L* standing for Latin, I have rather unwisely and indiscreetly mentioned to my father that one of my classmates whom I shall call Tim Morris (as that was very nearly his real name) is being pretty obnoxious to all of the Jewish boys including me. Worse still, he has a comrade and loyal ally whose name is Johnny, and together they both take considerable delight in making acerbic, hurtful and anti-Semitic jibes that are naturally and purposely directed at the Jewish members of the class of whom there are several and of whom I am just one. Though I am not physically threatened, it still worries me that Jewish boys are being picked upon in a particularly vitriolic and vindictive way. I am fearful that there may in due course be more than verbal aggression stored up for us one day very soon. This is my first and arguably my only personal experience of anti-Semitism, but I vividly recall how vulnerable I felt and how nervous I was - very nervous indeed. It was definitely not pleasant at all.

I suspect that these two lads can handle themselves appreciably better than their Jewish counterparts. We Jews were not born to fisticuffs and in truth rather meek by nature, maybe as a result of being parentally over-protected. We might watch a boxing match, but we are very much at arm's length – the voyeurs well away from any splatter of blood. We might be able to hold our own on a chessboard, or in an argument with rhetoric, but rarely in a schoolyard scrap. I felt very uneasy at the time and candidly admit that I was, to be blunt, an absolute blithering coward. I had not been brought up in the East End and had not therefore been taught how to fight back. My father had been born in Salford and in a different era - not one receptive to pandering. He is the recognized *'gaffer'* this day (if not every day), and is insistent that we should bring this sordid affair and these lads unacceptable behaviour to the immediate attention of the Head - a silver-haired yet rather kindly looking fellow with a pointed nose. I am reassured by father that he will hastily take peremptory action, and that this will prove to be a perfect example of **nipping it in the bud**, however prickly this particular rose might be. Father was - as they say - *focused.* Utterly and totally focused.

I am reassured by my dad that I need not worry.

I worry. In fact there's no denying it - I worry one heck of a lot.

If I voice my fears, he will bite my head off and so I keep these thoughts to myself. ***'Don't be such a softie'*** he would have told me. And looking back, quite right too. Oh for the benefit of hindsight and experience!

In the streets of the East End, Jews had defiantly defended themselves against the black shirted anti-Semites and had won widespread plaudits from their peers well beyond Cable Street or Petticoat Lane. On this particular occasion, my father is determined to emulate them by demonstrating that no one will call his son a '***Yid***' now or ever. I am shaking with trepidation and I almost wish that I had never mentioned this whole sordid matter to my father, as I am worrying about what may happen next. My stomach is churning with worry. I want to sink into a corner of oblivion. I visualise rolling the film back.

I feel nervous in anticipation of any future repercussions this action may have in my class. It is I, and not my determined father, who will have to face both Tim and Johnny in the classroom tomorrow morning, which daunting prospect is ***not*** filling me with any obvious feeling of jubilation. But nor does it appear to preoccupy father - who at all times remains resolute. He is seething and concentrating solely upon the objective he is pursuing with true vengeance. He is the defender of human rights well before the Human Rights Act was ever even contemplated. He is back on Cable Street fighting our own battle without compromise. He is going it alone but with feeble child in tow. I feel like a wimp. Because I am one.

I am self-conscious, and seriously considering the probability of personal humiliation but I am led demonstrably by an irate father and I choose to run with the idea - if for no other reason than I am offered no possible alternative. Like most things in my childhood, my father was not one to be blithely ignored. There was a clear division between the responsibilities of parent and child. He definitely knew his and I was told mine. I exaggerate slightly, of course.

As I now re-tell this particular tale, I cannot honestly remember what precise language was used when addressing the Headmaster on that fateful day, but I am convinced that my father would not have ever considered mincing his words. I was asked to clarify what specific words the offender(s) had used, and I rather sheepishly but dutifully spewed them out to the best of my recollection.

The impact is, as had been promised all along, spontaneously sweet. The educated Headmaster feigns incredulity as he is apparently outraged by such unacceptable utterances from two of his beloved pupils. Immediate action is promised. My father is insistent upon this and the Headmaster has clearly gathered that the man before him is not for turning. The two of them appear to understand one another and have a clear accord. This particular Jew is not going away and the Headmaster knows full well that he needs to get cracking on this - and clearly does so.

I assume that cocky Tim was called in to the ***beak*** (our nickname for the Head at the time) to be cross-examined regarding his racist behaviour and, genuine or not, the very next morning bright and early he offers me his ***profuse and heartfelt*** apologies which I readily and very graciously (if not a little timidly) accept. Put up to it by the beak or not, Tim does what Tim has to do, if only for self-preservation. Johnny plays a supportive role on the periphery and nods perfunctory assent at the appropriate moments. As if trained at R.A.D.A, the two of them clearly have no desire to be expelled and so bow to establishment pressure with considerable aplomb and conviction. They say what they are duty bound to say to me in a most articulate way and with what appears to be some element of actual sincerity. I am impressed and also visibly relieved. Peace reigns in the class and miraculously I feel like the victor. No blood. Not even any recriminations. The yid is in the winning corner despite all odds. Once again we Jews have survived and have done so by standing up for ourselves.

Oddly enough, Tim and I subsequently were to become good friends and I much preferred it that way. He was sufficiently bright to adopt a pragmatic approach, realizing that it was better to fall in line with the Jews rather than blurt out any of his private prejudices in future. He toed the party line. ***Who knows what he really thought?*** I will never know, but were I to ever meet him in my twilight years, I would not hesitate to ask him. I prefer to believe that he was not a Nick Griffin clone after all but was just a bit of a naughty boy. I must also concede that the Jewish boys were far from perfect either. I am far more accepting now of the fact that we all have our own set of prejudices emanating in the main from fear and ignorance. Tim was no different, and was probably far less sinister than I had imagined. And the Jewish clique - insular, protective, secretive probably didn't really help one jot either.

But my audacious dad did what my dad had to do and good on him. He got a knockdown without a single punch being thrown. It was a – result, that's for sure. He taught me a great deal about being Jewish that day.

I had been advised by several other schoolmates at the time that the school Sports Master at Stand, whose name was Hargreaves (nickname *'Haggis')*, was not terribly well disposed to Jews either. I must give him the benefit of the doubt however and put this down more to the Jewish cultural ineptitude at sport rather than any indiscriminate distaste for all Jews on Haggis's part.

Who knows what he thought either? Hargreaves was a Master at Stand for many years, though I assume that he will probably have died by now, and I for one wish him and his family no harm. Haggis knew only too well that the Jewish boys neither willingly climbed the rope even half way to the top, nor ever nearly finished cross-country without cheating. He might have wrongly concluded this was more than mere incompetence. Academic we might be, but I do not recall a single budding Sebastian Coe among my Jewish peers. There was certainly no *'Chariot of Fire'* among the Jewish boys at my school. There was an Abrahams not one like Harold. As I have already said, I once made it into the school cricket team as wicketkeeper, which was an amazing accomplishment in itself for a Jewish boy, though I have to admit it was very short lived. That leather ball was far too menacing for any aspiring Jewish sportsman and I could not help visualizing myself with no teeth - not a pleasant prospect. Big nose, no teeth, not for me. I just ducked and to be totally frank I was absolutely *flippin'* terrified. My cricketing honeymoon did not last that long at all. I was also once told that it was Haggis who had blocked my elevation to prefect in my final year at Stand, though this was no great loss to me or to the school. For all I know, he may have stuck the boot in over my blossoming cricket career but I somehow doubt that this was the case. I was no Brian Statham. Definitely not. I kept my teeth in place instead.

The tale of Tim Morris is relevant to my search for Jewish identity for a number of reasons. Firstly, I am assuming that he was merely copying the behaviour and attitudes that he had himself witnessed in his own home and emanating from his own parents. In his defence, he probably knew no different. My reaction nowadays is to educate and befriend rather than alienate altogether and this remains my motivation in building bridges among people of all religions and prejudices. I am sufficiently realistic to accept that many Jewish people have their own set of prejudices that also need addressing. Many of us of many beliefs do not embrace difference easily at all.

Secondly, my father had learned the lesson of history that Jews should no longer take it all lying down and that we must eventually fight our own battles. I was being taught by example and from an early age how we Jews need to stand up for ourselves. Though the year is circa 1965, many years later and despite a plethora of legislation, alarmingly little has changed. Prejudice against Jews, Moslems, Poles and Sikhs may be ameliorated by legislation but far from ever eliminated. Discrimination is dealt with by education and communication. We can make a real difference, but only if we first take a dispassionate look in the mirror. I try. We all have our own set of prejudices. We can easily feel uncomfortable with anything or anybody with whom we are not familiar. We need to fight against those negative instincts of human nature. We need to embrace difference. This is a real challenge in a fast moving, multicultural society like ours. Even within our own religions, we can be intolerant of one another, as I myself have already rather ashamedly admitted.

Thirdly and lastly, the ghetto mentality of ethnic groups like the Jews inevitably causes resentment and misunderstanding and similarly raises the fundamental issue as to where we draw the line on assimilation. As I have pointed out, the frum *Jews* strutting along the streets of North Manchester troubling no-one and other black-hatted bearded Jews on the East side of NY present me with a real dilemma. Part of me is proud but incongruously, an equal part of me is unarguably uncomfortable. Even at Stand, I wonder whether Tim resented the closeness of his Jewish classmates - our tribalism and our introspection. It can be a problem that, years later, I can now more readily understand and appreciate.

Drawing the line between integration and assimilation is a really awkward and thorny issue not only for Jews but for Sikhs, Moslems and many other ethnic groups as well. As I journey along, this is a haunting tune in my ear. There is much debate in this country and elsewhere regarding the turban on a motorbike or the former Foreign Secretary Jack Straw's aversion to the **burka**. There is much talk of banning religious symbols altogether at work or in other public places. To me, it is the thick end of the wedge and troubles me a great deal. Freedom to practice religion goes to the very root of who I am. My view is that the starting point must surely be that we can all dress in whatever we choose and practice our religion as we wish. We neither mean nor cause any harm. It is a dangerous road to go down and is at risk of becomes the proverbial ***'slippery pole.'***

I am also aware that prior to the Holocaust, German Jews became assimilated with great success but to no avail. I hope and believe that I am by nature tolerant. The wearing of special clothing and symbols, however unconventional, needs to be embraced, as the alternative is bigotry and tyranny. The burka, the black hat, the long black coat and the orange beard are all emblems and recognition and a celebration of personal choice. There are situations where exceptions have to be made, and the wearing of the burka by a defendant or a witness in a court case may well be a hindrance to justice, but these situations call for pragmatic sensitivity. They need to be very much the exception rather than the rule.

When my father intervenes at school, I am initially embarrassed by his absolute insistence upon making an example of my classmates. But I am also immensely proud of his determination to stand up for what is right and achieving an effective and timely outcome. All the Jewish boys in my class were to the best of my knowledge extremely grateful to my dad for his dynamic action in speedily establishing better relations between the Jewish boys and our school friends. It was indeed the time to stand up and be counted. The result was astounding and it taught me an important lesson.

When Oswald Moseley's henchmen were marching to the tune of Fascism, Jews were capable of fighting our corner when called upon to do so. The episode I have recounted was not violent but a fine example of fighting back by legal means. It was the lesson learned from Chamberlain's appeasement that was driving my father to pursue justice without one single moment's hesitation. He saw it as his parental duty to protect his son and his Jewish classmates from physical or psychological abuse. That was my father.

When the Israeli army shows its military mettle, it is driven and empowered by a similarly, gritty resolve borne out of an insatiable instinct for survival as well as a need to put the record straight. Jews have learned that in order to survive we cannot rely purely upon assimilation or passive acceptance, and nor (rather tragically) can we always rely upon others, whoever they may be.

For me, the story I have recounted as accurately as I can was a momentous victory and helped me to define who I am. I understood at a young and impressionable age of twelve that Jews are a group of people whatever our personal differences who come together - particularly at times of crisis, and that it is difficult for us to escape our Jewishness, as Hitler himself so adeptly demonstrated.

I have over the years come across many people who married out of the Jewish faith, only then to latterly return to their roots. I have known many others who have done so and have remained married happily ever after. For many though, it is as if there is a part of our self-conscious that inevitably pulls us back and the **Wandering Jew** dawdles back home. We **Wandering Jews** often return to our Jewish roots because this is our familiar territory and what our forebears have fought so hard for. I once suggested to a rabbi whom I knew pretty well at the time that he should adopt as a title for his next sermon the words used by the English national football team in the 2006 World Cup. He took up my suggestion and in a subsequent sermon that he gave he compared going to synagogue to '*coming home'*. I think that the words are apt in the circumstances and I was quietly flattered that he took up my suggestion. This is what it often feels like to me – being Jewish. When I hear a familiar tune in shule, I am - coming home. At a Jewish wedding or a bar mitzvah or a circumcision, I am deeply moved when I see the Jewish traditions maintained. This is where my heart is – in traditions and continuity and I am in a certain sense – '*coming home.*'

We are who we are and we are who we are born to be - and not necessarily who we *want* to be. My heartbeat pulsates to the Jewish tune, memories of that number stamped against their will on the arm of the unwilling inmate of the concentration camp, and the yellow star worn by every Jew religious or not. In the endless pogroms and in sight of the gas chambers, we were one people merged, if only by suffering. We supposedly chosen people have been kicked and stamped on indiscriminately in every era and in every part of the world. We need to sometimes kick back, and we jolly well do.

Recently whilst in Rhodes and visiting the one remaining Sephardic synagogue there, I saw a pitiful and heart wrenching photograph of a young boy whose name was Alexander. His coat bore the obligatory yellow Star of David, but one he apparently *chose* to wear as a celebration of his Jewishness. He had not been *ordered* to do so but it was his choice to do so and therefore a conscious act of defiance on his part.

A year or so later and this innocent child was rounded up with hundreds of Jews from the same island and carted off to Auschwitz where he was gassed to death. Of the sixteen hundred Jews who had been unceremoniously escorted to the camps from Rhodes, I read that one hundred and sixty two survived. It is hardly surprising that these events inevitably shape who I am and contribute to defining what being Jewish truly means to me. I know what human beings are capable of doing and regrettably I also know that evil knows no bounds. I read books about the Holocaust constantly and shed many, many tears. I cannot escape it. It is who I am. I never cease to be shocked or disgusted by such depravity. When I read of the Turkish barbarism towards the Armenians in the First World War, I am similarly outraged. Genocide is genocide, and any genocide is a tragic indictment of human nature in the gutter.

Partially for this reason, every Jewish boy at school took time off at our New Year if only to stand shoulder to shoulder with our Jewish classmates. This was not religion but kinship demonstrating the notion of a community - a theme to which I shall also return during the course of my journey.

When Jews are under threat, we are *all* vulnerable. Though there may be vast differences between us, there is an unspoken, ill-defined connection probably most apparent when we are under attack. I have admitted to an element of pride in winning an argument with Tim and his erstwhile accomplice. Though it was admittedly my father who fought this particular battle, all the Jewish lads in Form 2L were victors that day. There was a degree of self-satisfaction when the offending Morris was forced to grovel to me, maybe even against his will. But grovel he definitely did. It was by any definition a moral victory and a point well made. I admit that there was some mild cheering going on inside my buzzing head. I thought then, as I do so long afterwards, of **my dad - my hero** who was not for turning any other cheek. He told it as it was. It was a great lesson along life's journey.

No one should have to tolerate prejudice or humiliation whether on the basis of age, religion, sexuality, gender or colour. My Jewishness and in particular the true story which I have just recounted as faithfully as I can, has created my real desire to challenge those prejudices head on wherever they may manifest themselves even in my own backyard.

In the intervening years, some things have improved, but there is still considerable work left undone. There are laws but there are always those anxious to flout them. There are ingrained attitudes based upon one religious prejudice or another. There is ageism and there is sexism. There can be and too often is bigotry on both sides of the argument. There needs to be open and transparent dialogue on awkward subjects such as immigration, and there has to be moderation and compassion. We need to learn to respect difference and embrace it. I hear only this week of a young gay Jewish boy who took his own life in his teens apparently because his father couldn't deal with his son's sexuality. How tragic is that! A young son deprived of life and his parents losing a son forever. There has to be sensitivity and we have to think outside of that imaginary box.

As I have previously said, the effect of 9/11 has been devastating, as have the terrorist atrocities throughout the world, including my own home city of Manchester. The apparent rift between religions factions causes me real angst. Fighting prejudice is at the root of who I am and what being Jewish means to me. If we Jews cannot know the evil of prejudice - then *who*?

If not the Jew, who?

If we have genuinely been *'chosen'* for anything at all, it is surely to lead from the front in the fight against bigotry and any possible whiff of racism whatever its nature, and whoever is at risk of being hurt. Words and acts of anti-Semitism long pre-dated Tim Morris. Anti-Jewish fervour and vitriol have been around since ancient times. So too there is vile and vicious prejudice against immigrants in most countries of the world right now. Christians are under threat as are Moslems and Jews. No one is seemingly spared and I feel for them all as much as I feel for my own co-religionists. I feel for the innocent Palestinian caged in the refugee camp like an incarcerated lion at a zoo. Regardless of why they find themselves in that situation, it is just unacceptable and all of us stand guilty when anyone is forced to live in a state of demeaning misery. We must accept that something dreadful has gone wrong for this to happen. I am preoccupied with a sense of injustice borne out of the Jewish history of persecution and oppression, and this is an integral part of my own Jewish experience, and an inescapable aspect of my Jewish identity and who I am.

Pharaoh's order was apparently unequivocal: ***'Every son that is born to the Hebrews, you shall cast it into the Nile'***

Anti-Jewish sentiments were prevalent in the Greco-Roman world. This was duplicated in the Christian world, probably due to the conviction that the Jewish nation had directed people away from God's will. Anti-Semitism is not a modern phenomenon but immersed in religious claptrap and folklore. It is clear that Jews are perceived as the eternal enemy, and deep-rooted anti-Semitism has often been attributable to religious misconceptions and fanaticism.

In frantically searching for my own Jewish identity, I reflect upon the wanderings of the Jewish people as well as the relentless attacks both verbal and physical upon Jews. The nature, the frequency and the intensity of the incursions upon the rights and the freedoms of the Jewish people are bound to have had a profound effect upon me.

Anti-Semitism in its various guises defines who and what I am. It makes a vital statement regarding my Jewish identity. It causes me to be untrusting, often defensive and occasionally insular. All these various experiences make me philosophical, spending time looking for the true meaning of what evil really is, whether religion is the cause of conflict and what my personal Jewishness actually means. Can I exist perfectly adequately without it?

I only recently asked my mother which of her relatives perished in the Holocaust as the time had arrived when I needed to grieve for those whose voices I never heard and the faces I never saw. I think of the long lines of those chosen to work and those indiscriminately chosen to die. I think of the obnoxious chambers filled with Zykon B gas by deranged, heartless haters of humanity. This is total horror beyond my comprehension and I am haunted by it. It is small wonder that my Jewishness has been moulded by these catastrophic events. My allegiance must be to all those who were abused by the Germanic vilification of Jews and who were so powerless to resist. I remember all those poor souls who perished so needlessly and so sadistically in the name of ethnic cleansing and the final solution – designed to wipe them out, and almost succeeding.

But when I have delved further into the history of the Jewish people, I have been truly outraged at the depth and the extent of the endless hatred against the Jewish people. Our troubled history also brings with it a heavy burden upon Jews not to emulate our oppressors' bigotry. Prejudice is universally unacceptable and all racial or other discrimination absolutely disgusting. There can be no exceptions.

This is the very essence of my Jewishness – it represents a sense of real justice borne out of injustice, a duty to look outwards and beyond and to take something positive from the incessant anti-Jewish rhetoric and evil rants. We need to be vigilant in protecting and preserving human dignity. We need to have a heart and try our very best to feel other peoples' pain. As I constantly remind myself that *I need 'to walk in their shoes'*. Until then, I do not know.

Any notion that anti-Semitism began with Adolf Hitler is to ignore an appalling and disgraceful history of deep-rooted prejudice of a most vindictive nature over the course of many centuries. There has been a steady stream of Jew-baiters in every era. I recall, relatively recently, reading the obituary of Colin Jordan married to one of the Dior family and who lived and died a devoted disciple of Oswald Moseley. He was vehemently anti-Semitic and was at his most vocal during my own childhood years. Even today David Irving calmly articulates Holocaust denial. I once heard former BNP chief Nick Griffin try his best to conceal his hatred of Jews and blacks whilst smugly justifying repatriation. These are dangerous people who propagate the stereotype and trade in unadulterated hatred. They claim to be the custodians of what is truly British whilst unceremoniously decrying ethnic minorities. They do nothing for the English reputation other than to degrade it. They denigrate difference. Their jingoism conceals their evil and their intolerance. They whip up the vulnerable into a misguided frenzy.

Some years ago I wrote an article about the annual Holocaust Memorial day in which I suggested that it is the Jordans and the Mosleys of this world who need to be strapped to their seats in some plush city auditorium to hear a Holocaust survivor recount their story. We need to educate and to shock. To go on speaking about the Holocaust to Jewish audiences will not change anything, and so it has to be the perpetrators who must be compelled to listen. We need to educate and communicate with those who are dogmatically opposed to living in harmony with our neighbours of every origin.

So-called ethnic cleansing and racial massacres in Bosnia, Zimbabwe and Iraq demonstrate only too vividly that the world has actually learned very little from the Holocaust. In my own lifetime, and in my search for my own Jewish identity, this is the most distressing realisation of all. I try hard to feel the excruciating pain of the women repeatedly raped by ogres in Rwanda, or that of the innocent victims in Zimbabwe whose bodies are irreparably scarred by Mugabe's knives, whips and chains. There are tyrants throughout this world who go unchecked for far too long. Unless they have oil for us, the West seems to overlook them and literally let them get away with murder. Even the British government fails to recognise as genocide Turkey's treacherous treatment of the Armenians that I have mentioned earlier. There are some unforgiveable double standards at play here. Our hypocrisy is sometimes breath taking. As I journey along, I recognise this more and more.

The Jewish experience is not entirely unique as accounts of mass murder and racial disharmony continue to feature in the daily news bulletins to this day, but the declared intention to annihilate an entire ethnic group worldwide should make anyone shudder with absolute horror and revulsion. It is I believe without precedent. Every era has produced its own Jew haters ready and willing to blame the Jewish people for all manner of ills and afflictions. Jews are accused of just about everything. Curiously the common accusation is not that Jewish immigrants from Eastern Europe who generally had little money were scroungers. With Jews, it was generally quite the reverse. Jews were accused of being **too** powerful, **too** influential, and possessing the veiled intention of apparently ruling the world. For a relatively small ethnic group, I accept that we might well have exerted an unusually significant influence. We were involved in filmmaking, the press, banking and many other key commercial areas but to suggest that we had or indeed have any desire to rule the world is pure fantasy. This reverts back to my consideration of the stereotypical Jew. It can be and often is utter tosh.

The ferocity and venom of anti-Semitism is quite staggering. Born in the 1950s, it seemed to me that the Second World War was a million years in the past and that I was bound to be safe. I had never been in any air-raid shelter, nor has any bomb ever been dropped on my lawn. Just ten or so years earlier, the Nazis had been proudly pounding and stomping through the cobbled streets of Europe. But to me this was only history. The Holocaust was too ghastly to discuss openly and was not for young boys like me to hear about. It was never discussed at home and so far as I can recall we were never taught about it at school. It is regrettable that I remain ignorant of what really happened even to my own family. I was aware that my grandparents had immigrated to England from Eastern Europe before the First World War, but I had no real idea when and in what circumstances. My father was one of five children and had various relatives whom we met from time to time at family weddings and bar mitzvahs. But I was never told who was *not* there - and who had perished. It was an unspoken language. A subject barely touched. It was left to another day and locked away in a cupboard until the day never arrived.

Some few months ago, I spoke with my mother regarding our family secrets. She herself was born in England on the 6 July 1921. Her parents Eli and Sarah Knoll (nee Isaacs) originated from Russia and Poland. My grandpa had two brothers in England, one (Yankel) married in Manchester whilst the other (Max), a bit of a recluse, lived in London and never married. They may have had other siblings but if they did, they did not survive. I had not known my paternal grandmother who had died much earlier and only remember seeing dad's dad, also called Max, a few times before he died too when I was very young.

As to my great uncle Max, he came to stay with us occasionally but I cannot claim to have known him well. When he died many years ago, I experienced one of my life's most tragic events. I was the only person other than the rabbi at Max's funeral that was held at a cemetery in Walton Abbey. My mother had travelled to London the previous day to make the funeral arrangements for Max and I attended the funeral the next day on my own. The rabbi officiated and I duly responded '***Amen***' at the prescribed times. My mother's uncle was unceremoniously carted off and no one even blinked an eyelid. He led a solitary life and I witnessed his sad and pathetic ending. He was one Jew whom I suspect might well have forgotten his Jewish roots, and his lack of community left him entirely alone. He taught me a crucial lesson that I was never to forget, namely that we cannot and should not live in total isolation. Had Max been a member of a synagogue, he would have had a proper funeral and probably a ***minyan*** – a quorum comprising a minimum of ten men. This is the importance of ***Community***. I believe that most of us need to be part of 'something.' In my case, my something is my Jewishness.

I have already acknowledged that my father locked away many wartime secrets, not just of the girls he no doubt befriended on his army incursions into Europe but the impact Fascism was bound to have had upon him. He was on a cushy number, or so he always assured me. As a professional pianist in the army, he was consigned to playing in the band whilst serving in the Army Signals and was fortunately spared service on the frontline. Yet I am sure that he had informed my sister Marlene and I that he had been present at Bergen-Belsen at the time of its liberation. We never spoke about what he had seen there, but I have watched the newsreel narrated by the late Richard Dimbleby and witnessed even from a distance the horrors he would have seen. No doubt this had an enormous influence upon my father and might well explain his unerring determination to stamp out anti-Semitism whenever he became aware of it. These were horrors beyond words, evil beyond explanation and sheer hatred at total odds with humanity.

Anti-Semitism has, I am afraid to admit, helped to define who I am. It does not make me bitter, but more determined to do two things. To fight prejudice of any kind at all and secondly, never to spit in the face of those who fought to keep the Jewish race alive. Our survival is an integral part of who I now am. I remain the ultimate optimist who will always believe we can become better - by holding out our hand of friendship and educating those who want to be our enemies.

This is not however a book about anti-Semitism or the Holocaust but a journey in search of my own Jewish identity. This identity has been partially defined by what has happened to other Jewish people, particularly in times of extreme adversity. I have no desire to catalogue endless examples of anti-Semitism, but they cannot be entirely ignored in any attempt I make to describe who I now am.

In the fourteenth century, Jews were expelled from France, whilst Martin Luther in particular was constantly referring to Jews as an ***unwanted pestilence.*** I assume from this that he was not that keen on us.

Contemporaneously, anti-Jewish hostility had also spread across the Iberian Peninsula resulting in massacres in Spanish villages.

Meanwhile in Poland, Jewish communities were subject to constant attack, the consuls of Lvov in 1521 saying that ***the infidel Jews robbed us.***

In the 17th century, Jews were similarly forced to flee Brazil as a result of the Inquisition. It seems that only a few Jews have been spared the anti-Semite's wrath.

Though the emancipation of the Jews began towards the end of the 18th century in France, the book of the clergy of Colmar portrayed Jews in the most despicable and derogatory terms. More particularly in Alsace Jews under attack were forced to seek refuge in Switzerland.

Italian Jews were ordered to crowd into the ghetto and were deprived of their basic rights.

At the same time total exclusion took place in Lubeck.

In Frankfurt, Jews were forced to live in yet another ghetto.

The list of atrocities is almost endless and should you think it was any different here, I should add that in England in 1829 whilst Catholics were granted full civil rights, Jews were denied any such privileges.

In 19th century Germany, animosity towards Jews reached a crescendo with the anti-Jewish diatribes of Richard Wagner. Later in the same century, the Dreyfus affair in France provoked deep anti-Semitic fervour there as well. In Russia, there was a decree passed in 1882 forbidding Jews from settling in the countryside.

No, Hitler certainly did not invent anti-Semitism. He just extended its' scope and meaning well beyond any previous boundary.

There is unfortunately a recurring theme in Christianity that needs confronting. The fact that Jews are regarded as having the primary responsibility for the Crucifixion has been the justification for many examples of anti-Semitism. This religious intolerance has been the source of much bigotry and even during the Nazi era of World War Two the incumbent Pope was conspicuously silent and seemingly reluctant to speak out against Fascism. There is talk of some tacit support for the Nazis themselves, though this may not be accurately documented. Even today, the Jewish community in my own home city of Manchester has its own security from within our own community, tragically, but thankfully protecting Jews from acts of anti-Semitism and terrorism.

I am deeply affected by the Holocaust and my melancholy goes to the very heart of who I am. These monsters have destroyed the brothers and the sisters I never met and have consequently removed a part of me too.

It promotes a sense of outrage but also a sense of duty - not to have let these needless deaths occur in vain.

      I am not a victim but I am a survivor. I only survive because others have been victims. I therefore have a duty to pass on the mantle of Judaism to the next generation in order that they may make their own choices for their own futures. My survival brings its own set of obligations.

> ***Never to forget.***
> ***Never in my lifetime.***
> ***And I know that I never, ever will.***

CHAPTER SIX

THE CHOSEN JEW

"I'm Jewish. I don't work out. If God had wanted us to bend over, He would have put diamonds on the floor."

- **JOAN RIVERS**

The story goes as follows:

An old Jewish guy is praying at the Wailing Wall in Jerusalem's Old City. He bangs his chest time after time after time, repeating the same curious words incessantly:

'I vant to be with my people. I vant to be with my people'

And yet again he reiterates the same plea - in identical terms:

'I vant to be with my people.'

A *frummer* (a religious Jew), standing adjacent to him with his *tallit** (prayer shawl) neatly draped over his stained and creased jacket is fervently praying, but totally bemused by his co-religionist's pleas. Out of bewilderment, he is eventually compelled to tap his fellow Jew respectfully on the shoulder and gently plead with him as follows:

'Vot is this yer saying? I don't understand. Here you are - right slap bang in the middle of Israel at the Kotel (the Hebrew word for

the Wailing Wall) surrounded by hundreds of devout Jews and all you can say is: "I want to be with my people." You <u>are</u> with your people. Vot is your problem?'

Hearing this, he looks confused but says nothing to the religious Jew, but then whilst apparently ignoring him resumes his prayer:

'*I vant to be with my people. I vant to be with my people – in Monte Carlo.*' (I should say that the injection of certain 'letters' into the spoken word is intended to give the tale a degree of Eastern European authenticity.)

This reminds us that whilst many Jews regard their spiritual home as Israel, there are many more of us who prefer to bask in the sunshine of the Cote d'Azur rather than offer our prayers at the holiest site at the remnants of the old Temple. Putting it succinctly, being Jewish can mean many things to many people. We Jews are many people in many countries with many different aspirations. We are one people and yet we are not one at all. We are one ethnic group but comprise many facets. We are one religion but with numerous different beliefs. We have one God, though not all of us have discovered Him just yet. In other words, as with every other religion, Jews come in many shapes and sizes. As I have alluded to, the notion of an archetypical Jew is vastly over-emphasized and we need to be a little more guarded in our generalisations.

It is a relief that most of us laugh a lot too. And thankfully it is generally the case that Jews laugh, more than anything else, at us. Whilst we can be sensitive about non-Jews daring to be unduly critical of us, we love our own brand of self-deprecating humour highlighting the peculiarities of Jewish life as Jackie Mason has done over so many years so hilariously.

Jewish humour also helps to define who I am and who I like to be. I laugh at Jews a lot - particularly at our mannerisms, our peculiar idiosyncrasies and our relationship with non-Jews. We can be exceedingly funny and most frequently when we don't intend to be. I can find our hypocrisy absolutely jaw dropping, whilst at other times I regard our old-fashioned ways as particularly amusing. Our humorous ways make Jews who we are and reveal much about our character and about our fraught journey thus far. Amongst other things, our ethnic humour reflects our longstanding suffering, our deep sense of community and the Jewish character – our hypochondria, our paranoia and other similar perceived conditions attributed to us. I certainly take Jewish humour with me on my journey of discovery.

But Jewish life is not all about philosophy and religious edicts and there is ample time for us to smile as well. We all need some light relief and Jews are certainly no exception to this rule. After our historical experiences, we probably need more relief than most.

The language of 'Yiddish' is at the root of much of the finest Jewish humour. Many of its words are bastardized, whilst some others are actually quite uncouth. Some as with **schmuck*** for example are actually quite vulgar and understandably frowned upon, whilst others are just plainly embarrassing. But Jewish humour is without doubt another crucial aspect of my own blend of Jewishness. I am sure that even our jokes have been materially shaped by our traumatic Jewish journey with its many trials and tribulations. I do not confine this to the stand-up comic but to everyday Jewish life, where Jews laugh at many things, but as I have just said – primarily other Jews.

There have been many hilarious Jewish comedians over the years amongst whom I can recall Jack Benny, George Burns, Milton Berle, Sid Caesar, Joan Rivers and numerous others who have had much to joke about, adopting a common theme of self-criticism as they meticulously observe those recurring Jewish characteristics. Most Jews I know accept as a fact that we have some very unusually funny habits. Whether it is the notion of the Jewish princess placing onerous financial demands upon her helpless (but loyal) partner or the **mohel***, (the person who carries out the requisite surgery at the circumcision of a Jewish newly born boy) making ***a slip of a snip***, we laugh. I like to think that this willingness to be amused, particularly in a self-mocking way, has contributed in no small measure to our eventual survival.

We laugh at the stereotypical Jewish mother stinking the house out with ***gefilte fish****, or merely doting upon her children who can do no possible wrong. It is a distinct style of humour, once again setting us aside from our neighbours. It is a parody often based upon some harsh home truths. We are always willing to poke fun at the archetypal Jewish husband who is as unaccustomed to washing up the dishes as he is of doing any DIY. Jews develop buildings, but we don't generally build them with our own hands. I suspect that this is something to do with not getting our hands dirty. There has also probably never been a Jewish miner in the history of mining, and I feel sure that were we to ever be miners, we would probably only mine for diamonds and definitely not for coal. ***What money is there in coal for goodness sake?***

We do some jobs - but we definitely don't do others. This is yet again more a question of conditioning. For a Jew to change a car tyre is a major accomplishment. Whenever the Jewish husband changes a plug, it is his wife who tells him which is the negative, though even she is not entirely sure. The only time the car bonnet is opened is to show the AA man where the husband thinks the engine *may* be. The Jewish husband is not comfortable in the kitchen either and has been known to open the dishwasher door during its cycle only with dreadful consequences and some unwelcome flooding of the much-cherished terrazzo tiles. The wife is not pleased as she gets the mop out of the utility room. It is a long walk for her.

Things have moved on but only slowly. Nowadays, at least the Jewish husband will deign to carry the hoover down the stairs to enable his wife to plug it in. To a Jewish husband, an *iron* is a metal, and a *washer* is the little piece behind the screw. We know our place. It isn't so much we can't, as much as it is we just don't.

As with my attitude to the *shtreimel** the large trilby often covered in fur, I am sometimes hesitant about the use of Yiddish. I don't think I should be but I readily admit that I sometimes am. I love it for its richness and its depth, but I also recognize that it is stuck rather firmly in a time warp and associated with pogroms and ghettos. I am mysteriously concerned when I hear words of Yiddish being *borrowed* by the English language. I have listened to Jonathan Ross (whose wife I believe is herself Jewish) saying that he has *schlepped** around the shops with his wife. This appears to be a word now widely used by non-Jews. Suddenly I become possessive of something that on another day I am only too keen to deride. I become oddly protective as if we Jews actually own these words and the language itself. But, of course, we do. This element of 'double standards' appears to recur in many aspects of my attitude towards my Jewish identity. I fear I am that born-again hypocrite that our youngest daughter Dalia refers to (and regularly complains about.)

On Radio Four of all places, I hear erudite contributors to a rather highbrow discussion relying upon another common word of Yiddish – *tchotchkes**. Whilst I am proud that the English language has adopted one of our Yiddish words, I am also irritated that a word has been pilfered and a tiny fragment of our precious heritage has been hijacked. This is trespass if not treason to a Jew like me.

I visualise those helpless and desperate Jews cramped together in the overcrowded, typhus-filled bunkers of the extermination camps relying upon Yiddish as the only conceivable means of communicating with their fellow prisoners who have emanated from all parts of Europe. I suspect that this uniquely ethnic language played no small part in ensuring survival for more than the odd Jewish inmate. It was their survival kit in their demonstrably desperate circumstances. Yiddish is fading all right but is like a long lost family member and a vital part of the continuity of the Jewish people. It is and always will be a little part of me. Yiddish doubtless played its part in our emancipation, a secret code that our enemies could not understand and enabled us to communicate with one another in our darkest moments. It is a throwback to the ghettos into which so many Jews were thrown like bags of weather-beaten and battered potatoes. Yiddish at its purest is an inescapable part of who I am. I live in the present but part of me lives in the past. Rather inexplicably, I have a foot in both camps. As I just conceded, on a certain level I am horrendously guilty of some blatant double standards. ***Too Jewish – not Jewish enough. Proud to be Jewish. Almost ashamed to be Jewish. Why can I not be consistent for once?***

Without any doubt, Yiddish also provides a wealth of the very finest Jewish humour. We can be reluctant to use it nowadays as we have gradually become part of English society and prefer to leave mention of the shtetl well behind. Yiddish is still often spoken by the ultra-Orthodox who live their different life. This highlights my recurring theme of assimilation and integration. There are many words of Yiddish that are still actively in use. Remarkably, some words of Yiddish can express in a single word or two what would take at least one entire paragraph in English. The simple word ***noch**** is a good example of this. Literally translated, it means still or yet, though in practice it means a lot more. The words like ***taki**** and noch are four letter words that give emphasis to what has been said and are often tagged onto the end of the sentence as if only an afterthought. They are in their own unique way, magical words that can never be adequately translated into English. They are almost universally poignant, profound and pithy. Yiddish may well be the richest language ever created by man. There is a significant part of me that does not want to let such an expressive language perish being the language that my own parents would use in order to keep a conversation private and away from their children's' prying ears. It is a vital part of who I was then and who I am now. It connects the past with the present, the suffering with the survival. Many of these words of Yiddish are quintessentially Jewish and are unique remnants of a past and civilised age and a part of my multi-piece Jewish jigsaw - one that I am so anxious to piece together.

Yiddish is without doubt the funniest language in the world. And so here are a few random but memorable examples:

- ***acholera*** - is a curse meaning '*to hell with…*'

Apparently it might also mean that you wish ***cholera*** on the poor recipient too. Now that's some curse. Yet, believe it or not, it is said, not with any real venom but with rather endearing irony.

- ***eppes*** - can variously be translated as **'somebody,' 'perhaps', 'unsatisfactory'** or **'*quite'*.** It all depends upon its context, but is another favoured word of Yiddish that is once more slipped in just at the right moment. It means nothing really but says everything. How odd is that?

- ***farshtinkener*** - is translated as '***stinking'*** but is far more expressive than its English counterpart. It is a word that speaks what it means and is spat out rather than merely spoken. Whilst literally it means '***smelly',*** it takes on a wider meaning in practice as being applied to someone we are not terribly fond of or as we say in English – '***he stinks***.'

- ***rachmones*** - means '***pity'*** or '***compassion,'*** but again it means much more. It's a philosophy, rather than merely a word. It oozes compassion and expresses what we regard as a vital component of Jewish teaching, namely forgiveness.

- ***tateleh*** – this is a rich term of pure endearment that a father may use whilst addressing his young son. This is a word for which I have particular affection as my own father frequently addressed me as tateleh. I once had a letter from my father whilst I was at university addressed: '***Dear Tat'***. If only I could find that letter now as to me it was priceless.

This is just scratching the surface of the Yiddish language, but these words epitomize its uniqueness. There is so much more to find funny about Jews and about our Jewish way of life. Laughter is at the very epicentre of my Jewishness and were I ever to have married out of the Jewish faith, I believe that it is the lack of understanding of my sense of humour that might well have proved to be an eventual marriage-breaker.

Jewish humour is essentially ethnic and is at the very core of who I am. It is rich in history and deep in heritage, revealing much about how we Jews think. Our sense of humour reflects Jewish life and Jewish values. It speaks of parents over protecting their children. It touches upon the Jewish woman's exaggerated obsession with diamonds. It refers to Jewish hypochondria, and it frequently refers to Jewish business acumen and our obsession with success. It addresses Jewish relations with other religions, our eating habits and our moderate alcohol intake. It parodies the various generations of Jews and it highlights our own stereotypes. The less religious poke fun at more religious Jews, and we even laugh at the way we express ourselves. What can be funnier than the phrase: *'I want **that** you should be happy'?* The simple insertion of the word '***that***' tells us that the person who spoke those words is almost certainly a Jewish person of Eastern Europe extraction.

We refer to the use of '*vot*', instead of 'what. 'We use the word '*oy'* with ease. It seems that every Jewish husband is called Abie or Hymie and every Jewish wife is known as Sadie. This misrepresents who we truly are, though it can still be terribly funny. I have incidentally met a few Hymies in my time but never one single Sadie, at least to date. Maybe, just maybe, one day I will meet a Sadie and if I do, I will smile to myself, though hopefully she will not notice. I will be laughing ***with*** her of course and not ***at*** her.

I find myself frequently laughing to myself at my fellow Jews. For example, at **Yom tov** and at **Rosh Hashanah** (the Jewish New Year) in particular, Jewish men and women dash to the synagogue like it's a half marathon. Nowhere near the place throughout the entire year, we suddenly become obsessed with God's presence as He decides whether our name shall be in the Book of Life - or not. I refer to this by reference to my favourite word of all words: '***busying'***. Something somewhere pricks our conscience and just in case God is actually there after all, we go running to shule. We take a punt. Should God be watching us, I am confident that He will be smiling to himself. Many of us imagine that we can do a 'deal' with God, almost akin to doing a deal in business. Somehow I don't think so. He presumably knows the outcome in advance and, if there were ever a good businessman, it would surely be God himself. He certainly knew how to switch the lights on and darn well keep them on, as well as create the odd world here or there - no mean achievement in itself. Now there's real talent for you.

When a child makes some noise in the synagogue, which almost invariably occurs throughout every single Orthodox religious service I have ever attended, the elders of the congregation make an even greater din with the declared intention of encouraging the youngster to be quiet. Not a chance.

'***Shush ....Shush......'*** is screeched at the offending infant by the well-intentioned but interfering adults in question who have the sole intention of demonstrating their huge influence among their peers. After a lull of a minute or so at the most, the boisterous child begins to run around again, now creating as much bedlam as before and precisely nothing changes. This is a pointless Jewish ritual that I have witnessed time and time again, ever since the days when I was a child myself running around Heaton Park synagogue until my father gently grabbed me by the wrist and took me back to the seat adjacent to his. Jack wasn't for messing - as you will have previously gathered by now. Never violent I should add but extremely and pretty effectively assertive. This is what was called in my day – discipline. It can be quite handy in controlling one's children and used in moderation can be terribly effective.

It is part of our culture among the middle ground of Orthodox Jews in particular that we go to synagogue to talk. We go there for what in Yiddish is referred to as a good *yachne**, namely a 'chinwag.' I defy any other religion to behave like this. It seems, more often than not, that praying is merely an incidental by-product and little else. The prayers are almost inaudible because of the incessant chatter, but we enjoy the experience of being together and catching up. For most, the truth is that we go to 'say' not 'pray.' I occasionally ask myself, when did I last see a quiet Jew? I am struggling to remember. In fairness, it does not help that prayers are almost always recited in Hebrew, a language still foreign to most of us, even after all these years. This goes back to our cheder days I referred to earlier. We learned to say but not to understand.

The fact is that we just prefer to talk. We listen a little, but we talk a great deal and I confess that I am no exception. I pretend to listen but I mean to talk about all manner of everyday things. In orthodox company, I have heard it said that if you want to pray, you should go to the Reform *shule*. Our Orthodox synagogues are mostly convivial places where old friends meet and the current economic situation is carefully scrutinized. This is a religion built upon communal discourse rather than silent prayer. We argue about politics rather than about the *sedra**, the weekly portion of the reading of the Torah. We are what might be referred to as cultural Jews - where fraternity is more sought after than strict religiosity. It is built firmly upon the foundation of **Community.**

On ***Yom Yippur**** (the yearly fast day) there are many Jews I know including myself who genuinely fast all day. I suspect that there are many more who ***claim*** to fast than actually do. When the rabbi comes over to them, they get ***busy*** again, trying to impress their bearded leader and mentor that they are rather suddenly devout and observant. I am wondering to myself why someone went home in the middle of the service if not for lunch. But they look pale and drawn as the day rolls on and convince themselves (and sometimes me too) that they have really been fasting all day long after all. In the end, I choose to believe them, though I have my niggling suspicions. Some congregants ask how long there is to go before the fast ends in order, no doubt, to add credence to their charade. In order to perfect the account, they finally ask my brother in law Jack Maurer, a kosher baker in his time, whether he has smuggled in some bagels for them to munch on. As well as being funny, Jews can be terribly predictable. But it is good, clean, inoffensive fun. It is what Dawkins might call a delusion. Though I must make it clear that the Jewish humour is for real and definitely not illusory. Jewish belief may be an illusion but certainly not Jewish humour, which has deservedly earned a reputation for longevity. As to fasting, the Jewish approach is based upon fear, habit and culture. To what extent is it really down to religion? I'm not entirely sure. The jury has to be out on that one too.

One prayer in particular demands that, during its silent recital over the High Holy Days, the chest must be banged pretty robustly and close to where the heart hopefully beats. This is perfected with a clenched fist in order to presumably signify true conviction. I look around the synagogue as this prayer unfolds. Some bang so hard that they are at risk of breaking their fragile rib cage. This makes good theatre and probably clears their phlegm in the bargain too. Some congregants love this prayer; I see it in their fists. It is a prayer specifically designed for the extrovert and absolutely perfect for the born-again Jew. What more telling example of religious conviction than self-harming? This is akin to Abraham's sacrifice of a son in biblical times. This is a golden opportunity to shine among your clutch of Jewish friends. The more we bang, the more we apparently know our stuff. I laugh out loud but retain it inside my head.

For some peculiar reason, I myself refrain from even gently tapping my rather slight chest lest I prompt a coronary. I am the outsider again. Self-inflicting pain on my chest is not something that comes naturally to me. As with the habitual swinging back and forth during prayer, which is apparently indicative of concentration, I remain purposely detached and conduct whatever meagre prayers I have to offer - motionless. I prefer to be a little more subtle than that. I recall my father would always be disparaging towards those who made a big show of praying. Like him, I rebel against all this high drama. I am, as is often the case, the loner on the periphery and the rebel in my own camp. As part of my Jewish identity – I am the Jewish outsider/insider. One foot in – another foot out. Possibly the best of both worlds and none.

In Yiddish, they would say that I am *eingeshpart**(always looking for an argument)**.** In English, it might be said that I am being awkward for awkward sake. But the fact is that I just find it all too self-indulgent and hysterically hypocritical. I prefer to keep my prayers to myself and, as I have just made clear, my father was similarly disposed. My view is that these overtly ostentatious signs of religious fervour need to be treated with some circumspection. The letters 'O' – 'T' and 'T' come to mind, if you follow my meaning.

When the Priests (known as the **Kohanim***) give their priestly blessings in shule, the rest of the congregation are obliged to keep their eyes looking down and not at them. There are those who, in order to impress others that they really know exactly what to do, yet again make a real song and dance of this. They put their tallit over their head and purposely and overtly turn their back on the Priests. In other words **'I know my stuff.'** It makes for a great performance, especially by those who go to the synagogue once a year but love to make a big show. I smile to myself at moments like these, though hopefully they have not noticed. I don't go for ostentatious prayer, that's for sure. When it comes to prayer, I prefer a little modesty.

I have already described the migration of Jews from Eastern Europe to England and elsewhere, as well as the movement of those same Jews from town to country. In my own city of Manchester, there is a stark and truly amusing example of this. I am constantly chuckling at what I witness. The same Jews who once had their humble habitat in Crumpsall or Strangeways close to the inner city centre move to more rural areas such as Hale or Bowdon in Cheshire. These areas are close to Manchester airport on the South of the city. As our people gravitate to more areas, they can in a sudden fit of amnesia entirely forget where they had until very recently lived. In the same way that anti-Semites spit out the word **Jew,** rather than use the same word with any possible affection, many of my revered co-religionists spew out the words **North Manchester** as if there were an imaginary border crossing or toll at the centre of Manchester's Albert Square. Jews are funny like this. They may be no funnier than non-Jewish people who have done well, but they are nevertheless more hilarious than they will ever know.

Manchester is a relatively small conurbation and the journey to upper class suburbia is just a half an hour's drive away. It is a real pity that they create this enormous gulf between where they are now and where only yesterday they once so proudly belonged. I am sure this is not uniquely Jewish but to me it remains a source of real amusement. Though my father had moved the family to Whitefield, which in those days represented a similar move **upwards**, he would forever remind us that he had been brought up in Strangeways and educated at Salford Grammar. I always knew we had come from humble roots and never saw any reason to be ashamed (indeed quite the reverse). Dad did well at one stage and undoubtedly liked to show off a lot, but he never hid his working class background. That is an absolutely fundamental aspect of my Jewishness. No man or woman is more important than the next, regardless of colour, creed, age, sexual orientation or wealth. These were the days when most Jews voted labour – being socialists at heart. A key word in my own vocabulary is 'opportunity' and every one is entitled to that. The tragedy is that far too many decent people never get an opportunity at all.

In my mind we were all from the ***haim*** * which literally means 'home', though referring to the shtetls in Eastern Europe. When any human being thinks that he is more special than the next man, I spot real danger. The current trend towards an obsession with celebrity is symptomatic of this, and is illusory. There are many Jewish jokes concerning this attitude. They parody the attempt by many Jews to make a break with the past – be it Yiddish or their former less salubrious place of residence. They are in denial. But what is far more humorous is that next sequel of the story to which I have referred. In order to escape the North Manchester ghetto, Jews move **exceedingly** far afield, some 18 miles up the road no less to Cheshire, for example, as I have just mentioned. They feel hemmed in by the close proximity of the houses, the multitude of big black hats and the overly and overtly Jewish neighbourhood. I am sympathetic to these sentiments, as it can indeed be stifling sometimes.

These Jews hurriedly and frantically head off for rural England, where they can enjoy the English summers, rolling hills and cream teas and where they are able to watch from their balcony non-Jews going for long walks. As they make their escape from ethnic congestion, they are heard to say with some considerable relief that they have discovered their welcome oasis. They have escaped the Jewish ghetto. They are becoming properly 'anglicised.'

The trouble is that they have not anticipated what occurs next. As the Jewish population of Southport, Lytham St Annes and many areas of North Manchester, fill their removal vans with their treasured capo di Monte and other precious and prized belongings for onward dispatch to spacious Cheshire, new resplendent synagogues are soon built to accommodate all the newcomers. New shops are opened with full fanfare selling Judaic wares and a full range of kosher food to these English Jewish settlers. In due course there are spotted, in the precise area where they have moved to, horror of horrors but surely not. Yes, big black hats, long black coats, tailored beards and hanging curls, shuffling along their sacred Cheshire walkways making their way to the local synagogue. Sadie lifts her hands up in utter despair, fearing that surely they must have taken a wrong turning off the M sixty something motorway. She is almost distraught at the prospect of a fresh influx of frummers encroaching upon her newly acquired rural space. There appears to be no escape as these new Jews are being stalked by the ultra-religious. Sadie begins to believe that she is being pursued by God's henchmen and dawdles, somewhat deflated, into her huge kitchen diner in order to contemplate her next move. She cannot stay here a minute longer. It's just all too much of the same – too Jewish.

In our haste to escape, we Jews soon create a new Jewish ghetto, inevitably underpinned by a minimum of two brand new synagogues, a fine array of communal organisations and a plethora of more conventional Jews from North Manchester who now unashamedly wander around the area as if they belong in rural England too. There is no escape and these emancipated Jews are doomed and resign themselves to the fact that they are forced to share the Cheshire countryside with other Jews who wear their Jewishness for all to see. Nothing has changed after all, other than the view. Jewish life cannot and will never be extinguished by others or by us. I should add that the newly constructed synagogues in the areas I have just mentioned are actually flourishing as history yet again repeats itself and the Wandering Jews continue our journey, be it up market or not.

The mind boggles as to where the escapees are bound for next. I have in mind Congleton in the depths of Cheshire, where in its entire history, rather like Rhyl, not one single Jew has probably ever settled and not that many will have even passed through. They should be safe there for a while, at least until the Jewish entourage moves on again with its customary determination to escape - only then to build a brand new, bustling community all over again. This is Jewish evolution visibly at play. Mancunian Jews have moved, and Jewish life has followed them. This will, no doubt, be similar throughout England and beyond. Golders Green, Finchley, Hampstead Garden suburbs. There is no easy escape here either. Leeds to Harrogate; Hull to Leeds; London to Hertfordshire and so forth. I have no definitive proof but I assume that this is what happens worldwide to every Jewish community in every country. However hard we try to extricate ourselves from the constraints of our past, the wanderers are destined to return. We are the eternal Wandering Jews and there appears to be no realistic escape. You may find a home in a faraway enclave but Lubavitch will find you. Because this is who I am. The Israelites. The Tribe. The Wandering Jews.

There will always be some very anglicised Jews who do manage to escape to Buckinghamshire where they are able to assume a fresh identity, change their surname to Summers-Smith in order to avoid all references to Goldberg, and live an authentically English life. They will go for walks in Great Missenden and just a little uneasily drink shandy at the local public house. They may even take up pool. But these Jews know they have left a little part of themselves at home and eventually many, not all of course, will wander back home. Like me, they want the best of all worlds. But they just can't get the Jewish bit totally out of them. They are in disguise but their Jewishness has taken deep root.

As I will mention as I journey further along my way, it is hard for those who want to divest themselves entirely of their Jewish identity. Like Rock from Blackpool, the word *Jew* runs *through* our veins, however adamant some of us try to shake it off. We may not want to be *too Jewish,* but generally speaking, we still want to be Jewish. I may not always want to pray at shule, but I still need to be *near* one. I may regard Yiddish as embarrassing, but it remains part of me and I am afraid to let it go entirely. I may look with disdain at huge black hats and curly locks, but I still accept that this is a part of me too.

The synagogue itself actually spawns endless funny situations. When I see the vast and lavish headgear worn by some of our women as they nonchalantly walk along the road on their way to shule on a Shabbat morning, I wonder what non-Jews will be thinking of us. As I pass the lines of cars parked in the roads nearby, but not too near so as to offend the rabbi, I smile to myself and can visualise the rabbi turning the other cheek from beneath his own expansive fedora. I shake hands with the security man currently on guard at the synagogue's gates whilst protecting us from terrorists. I am keenly aware of our vulnerable predicament in current times. It is all fancy hats and Israeli security firms that make for an incongruous juxtaposition but a reminder that we are still constantly under threat from anti-Semitic forces in our midst, post 9/11.

Jewish security within our own community is big, necessary and serious business. In addition to security men, members of our own congregation are on their homespun security rota. As they stand outside the front gates of the synagogue, I have often wondered what they would actually do if, God forbid, there was ever to be a real emergency. I suspect that they would be tempted to secure their own escape and take a dash for it and I am not sure I could ever blame them. Self-preservation is a persuasive human instinct as history has demonstrated many times before.

Inside the synagogue, there is much more to keep me firmly amused. There are some who come to pray but appreciably more, as I have said, who are in shule for other reasons. David, a regular and loyal congregant, leaves the synagogue before noon and well before the end of the service in order that he might go to the gym. He has never ever been known to pick up a prayer book, though he attends *religiously* every single morning. He is by all accounts more partial to picking up weights than any prayer book, and yet he has an almost uncontrollable urge just to be there. ***Loyal as the day is long but to what and to whom?***

On a Sabbath morning, there may be 120 people attending the morning service, whilst at Yom tov, the synagogue is positively heaving. On the High Holy Days, the rabbi's sermon seeks to encourage greater observance in the forthcoming year, though in his heart of hearts he knows full well that his words have little if any enduring impact at all. The bulging numbers rapidly dwindle to normal proportions almost immediately after the service is concluded. He must however be seen by his congregants to be trying hard; this is his job - to exhort others to become God fearing. In the Jewish world, as in most of the world generally, this can be one uphill struggle in a secular world.

The relationship between family members is another source of good, clean, Jewish fun. The Jewish student going to university with no idea how to clean a dish; the mother **kvetching*** at every conceivable obstruction in her way, however insignificant; the relationship between Jewish husband and wife in which the wife takes on all domestic tasks other than those she can delegate to her maid or one of her cleaners.

Jewish habits can and do keep me constantly amused. The words we use and the actions we take are often entirely attributable to the fact that we are Jewish. But also sometimes equally funny can be the attitude of non-Jews towards Jews. So here's a memorable example of my own.

I was about 10 years of age and playing pitch and putt with dad in Rhyl, then a rather rundown seaside town in North Wales close to Colwyn Bay. It is one of those many places where Jews just don't generally go. This was true 40 years ago and to the best of my knowledge probably remains the case today. As my dad and I played some serious mini-golf, my mother, as dutiful as ever, waited patiently in a multi-coloured wooden hut adjacent to the last green. When the game was over, all three of us went off arm in arm along the breezy, somewhat tawdry promenade. It was only at this stage that my mother revealed to us what words had been spoken in that sacred shed whilst we had been busily preoccupied with our mini-golf.

It was best recounted once a certain old lady was well out of sight. Mum had apparently met this elderly Welsh lady who sat opposite her in the chalet-type hut. She started chatting and politely asked my mother whether she liked Rhyl. My mother apparently white-lied and said:

'Yes, it's lovely' 'and you?' she hesitantly reciprocated. The Welsh lady took a deep, long hard breath and, after only momentary deliberation, replied - with a pronounced Welsh twang:

'It's all right' she said *'but'* (and hesitating for a moment, she added*)*
' It's all fish and chips and - Jews.'

My mother was silent but apparently nodded affably. She was not in the mood for boxing or even for any verbal tirade. When the story was re-told, all three of us (to use the modern vernacular) laughed out loud. I think my dad suggested that my mother ought to have responded with a little tinge of outrage, but even he was aware that he was in dreamland. We both knew my mum better than that. We all three had a good laugh about this old lady's wholly inaccurate description of Rhyl, borne out of deep-rooted, maybe harmless, prejudice. The fact is that we were probably the only three Jews to visit Rhyl that day but this was clearly this lady's stock phrase. She regarded fish and chips as *'common'* and Jews as *'unwelcome visitors'*. She would not be unique. Whether that still applies to Rhyl today, I cannot be sure, but we three certainly had to giggle. Had she said it to my father, the tale might well have ended quite differently. You know jack like I know Jack.

Jewish people are not by nature or inclination rural people. We like some of the seaside, but not all. We have taken a shine to Lytham St Annes and to Brighton and Hove, but there are few Jews in Morecambe for example. We are not big hitchhikers, but we are perennial shoppers. We are not farmers, as we do not drive tractors, but only 4 x 4s. We visit the Lake District or the Yorkshire Dales, but only for short bursts. We live in Leeds but not in Huddersfield, Manchester but not Burnley. Brighton but not Hastings, Hull but not Grimsby. As I have said, we are tribal. I generalise a little too much but you get the flavour.

We are truly ethnic too. Like some other religious groups, we move en masse. As I have previously described, we may not enter the shule for praying purposes too regularly but nevertheless most of us want to be not *too* far away.

Inter-marriage is another subject - all on its own but suffice to say there remains a driving urge on the part of many Jews to preserve our culture and our religion. Though inter-marriage happens with regularity, there are many Jews who regard it as one of the cardinal sins. We have heard of excommunication and many tears shed. I own up to believing that the Jewish people should live on, and I accept that marriage out of the faith is by its nature at risk of diluting it. This is another aspect of the funny side of Jewish life. Everyone has an opinion. One likes the rabbi, the next one despises him. One eats kosher, the other one doesn't. Every Jewish person is convinced that he is right. This can be a dangerous trend.

These different opinions can also be the cause of major rifts and familial discord. Take the case of a loyal and devoted son whom we shall call Michael and who has been brought up in a moderately religious household. He sets off on a trip to Israel with a Zionist youth group, much to his parents' great delight. But he comes back home **transformed**. He has been struck, not with lightening, but with the frummer bug. Initially his parents, Monty and Lottie, are pleased: '**Better that he should become more religious than marry out**' his relieved mother is heard to remark, whilst seated comfortably in her Poggenpohl kitchen-diner. But over a period of time, their initial delight wanes. Every Shabbos, **Michel** (formerly Michael) insists that no light is switched on or off, no football results read out, no motor vehicle driven and shule on Saturday morning now begins at 9.30am, and not 11.30 like in the old days last month.

To Monty, this is a brand new world but Monty is not brave. The parents become gradually irritated, whilst **Michel** feels uncomfortable about the standards of his mother's **kashrut*** (kosher eating) in the home. They are no longer strict enough for his liking. What seemed to be a dream has soon turned into a total nightmare for Lottie in particular who feels like her kitchen is no longer her own. There is heard the audible sound of friction as these shades of religious orthodoxy clash like Buddy Rich's cymbals once did. Family civility is firmly put at risk of serious disruption.

I am also often amused by Jewish ritual and customs of which I now offer up one or two random examples. When there is bereavement within the Jewish community, there is frantic activity. People who haven't seen the deceased for years converge upon the house of mourning with appropriately long faces and bleary eyes. Photographs are covered over as is the Jewish custom, and a candle on the table burns respectfully in memory. The mourners sit on low chairs, so they may be near **terra firma** where the deceased has recently been buried. These Jewish visitors form orderly queues at the door and are noisily nudging forward in their desperate insistence upon being noticed. They churn out the words that they have heard others use many times before: '**I wish you Long Life**' (the customary Jewish words to the mourner) and famously: '**we should only meet on simchas*** (happy occasions) or the abbreviated version which has become more recently popularized: 'simchas.' My word – **busying** – comes to mind again.

There is much *shockling* (swaying back and forth in prayer) as the prayers kick off good and proper. The inconspicuous women sit silently and deferentially in another room whilst the male throng pretends to pray, though once again in the obligatory foreign language. There is much muttering. The ladies are relegated to the side benches, which I do find terribly demeaning, even after all these years of watching this going on. The men predominantly pretend to pray whilst the women look down towards the ground in communal solemnity. This is what the good book ordains, though difficult to reconcile in modern times when we purport to strive so hard for some element of equality. I am informed that this is what the Torah deigns. It's what the Good Lord has said and, therefore, it shall come to pass. We are after all the Orthodox cavalry, whose role is to rebel against any talk of Reform. No change in this shop.

Conversation at the *shiva** house soon shifts to the most pressing matters of all. Manchester United, the price of kosher food, the rabbi's shortcomings and as ever, the rise of anti-Semitism. There is an abundance of rushing and pushing as hands are shaken, offering the immediate family much needed solace and sympathy. At these times, we Jews feel part of something – a clan. A cacophony too.

Most mean well and I am not cynical enough to believe that there is no genuine grief among the mourners, but I do wonder whether a sense of duty is the driving force as much as genuine empathy. Occasionally I fear it is just another Jewish occasion when Jews come together to be overtly Jewish once more. These rituals are important if only to remind us all who we actually are. To be brutally honest, there is nothing quite like a disaster to bring Jews together. It's the familiarity of these rituals that make them so tribally attractive and special. To be part can be preferable most times to total isolation.

At a shiva house, the noise can be shrill but this is an integral part of our Jewish culture. As we talk in the synagogue, so we talk at cemeteries and in houses of mourning. I smile to myself at the thought of everyone talking about everyday things that really don't matter, especially on such solemn occasions as these. But these Jews really don't mean any harm. I smile inwardly as this is as I well know by now exactly who we are. We talk incessantly and often at the most inopportune times about terribly inconsequential things.

There are a multitude of Jewish jokes on every conceivable subject of which I have chosen the following ones, purely by way of example. They are brief, hopefully inoffensive and indicative of what being Jewish actually means to me.

- The waiter turns to the group of Jewish female diners at his table and asks: *'Is **anything** all right?'*

- The young Jewish child tells his mum proudly that he has a part in the school play. She asks what part he plays, to which he replies: **'A Jewish husband.'** Mother is unusually downhearted. She pleads with the son: **'Go back to the teacher – insist you want a speaking part.'**

- The question is asked: ***How do we know Jesus was Jewish?*** The answer is apparently obvious:

'He lived at home till he was 30, went into his father's business, and his mother thought he was God!'

- The Jewish mother sees her adult son falling into the lake. She screams hysterically:

*'**Help, help, my son, the doctor, is drowning.**'*

And finally:

- ***What do Jewish wives make for dinner?***

Answer; ***'Reservations.'***

These jokes, playful and harmless though they may be, are symptomatic of what Jews are perceived as being – protective, dutiful, demanding and funnier than we ever ourselves imagined. Even these jokes are a part of who I am. They are innocuous, inoffensive and hark back to my days of innocence in our cul-de-sac in Crumpsall when I thought the entire world was Jewish and life was eternal.

Being Jewish can be serious stuff, but it can also be jolly funny. The recurring theme of Jewish humour appears to be self-deprecation, which is one of the more attractive aspects of Jewish life. We laugh at ourselves a lot, presumably because there is a lot to laugh at. With a history predominantly marked by suffering, it is a source of great comfort to laugh - and to be able to laugh at us.

We Jews are renowned for making fun of ourselves - and may it long continue. Jewish humour is an essential part of who we are and who I definitely am. It's good that we can see the funny side, especially of our own people. It serves to underpin our innate tribalism, and each of those jokes I have just re-told on my journey definitely make me laugh out loud. I cry a lot, but thankfully – I laugh a lot too.

- **TALLIT** is a prayer shawl with fringes worn in synagogue for certain services.

- **SCHMUCK** Please forgive me for this one, but it comes from the Yiddish 'schmok' meaning penis. Not a word my mother likes me to use!

- **MOHEL** is a Hebrew word for the Jew trained in the practice of the covenant of circumcision.

- **GEFILTE FISH** is a traditional Ashkenazi dish – either boiled or fried, and formed into fish balls or patties. If you have never tried it (and every Jewish person I know certainly has), you have missed a real treat. Often enhanced further by the addition of **'chrain,'** otherwise known as horseradish sauce.

- **SHTREIMEL** is a fur hat worn by married Hasidic Jewish men on the Sabbath, and during other festivals, though I seem to see them worn at other times too.

- **SCHLEPP** is an interesting Yiddish word and, as I have mentioned, one widely adopted in the English world. Whilst on the one hand, it means dragging yourself, or someone else, somewhere, and inferring it is a long way to get there, it also denotes the noun **'Schlepper'** who drags his heels - and is something of a 'loser.'

- **TCHOTCHKES** is a curious word to read, and means a bauble or a knick knack with little or no functional use.

- **NOCH** cannot really be properly defined but as best as I can – Not, yet, more. Impossible for me to help on this one.

- **TAKI** is, as with noch above, impossible to define without context. It is a word that almost means nothing on its own but can be a way of emphasizing the remainder of the sentence.

- **ACHOLERA** of a word of similar spelling in the Yiddish way of wishing a plague on someone. Positively charming!

- **EPPES** means a little, not much.

- **FARSHTUNKENER** is a stinker.

- **RACHMONES** is defined as pity.

- **TATELEH** is an endearing term for someone you love. In fact 'tate' is the dad and tateleh the diminutive.

- **YOM TOV** means Jewish holiday/Jewish festival.

- **ROSH HASHANAH** is the Jewish New Year. Two days of Rosh Hashanah and a week later the day of Atonement, Yom Kippur.

- **YACHNE** is translated as a gossip or a busybody.

- **SEDRA** is the particular portion of the Torah recited that particular week.

- **YOM KIPPUR** is the Day of Atonement when Jews fast from the eve of Yom Kippur to sunset on the actual day. No food, no drink. It makes you think. If only of food.

- **EINGERSHPART,** I believe, is meaning awkward or cantankerous.

- **KOHANIM** are the Priests. Those with the surname Cohen are I believe Kohanim, and are of direct patrilineal descent from the biblical Aaron.

- **HAIM** means literally – Home - but in its proper context refers to our original homes in Eastern Europe – Back in the Haim.

- **KVETCHING** is another word adopted by the English language, but is intending to signify constant moaning and complaining.

- **KASHRUT** refers to the kosher dietary laws that include separation of milk and meat, and the ban on certain meats and all shellfish, but also requires slaughter according to Jewish ritual.

- **SIMCHA,** as a noun, means a Jewish party or celebration - but literally is a Hebrew word meaning 'Joy.'

- **SHIVA** is the weeklong period of mourning the death of a father, mother, son, daughter, brother, sister or spouse. The word Shiva means seven. The mourners sit on chairs low to the ground.

CHAPTER SEVEN

JEWISH CEREMONIAL

"Man's main task in Life is to give Birth to himself, to become what he potentially is. The most important product of his effort is his own personality."

- **ERICH FROMM**

In the Jewish world, we tend to congregate in our own sometimes-congested communities. They were in a former epoch referred to as ***ghettos***. And so it is perfectly natural that family announcements in the various Jewish newspapers, such as the Jewish Telegraph up North or the Jewish Chronicle in the South of England, are bound to be a vital and obligatory part of the weekly reading for many of us in the Jewish community.

As a matter of course, I read the obituaries, the births and the marriages before catching up on the more mundane issues affecting daily Jewish life in an otherwise generally insignificant period of seven days. I value these moments, some sad and others happy, as they are once again an intrinsic part of who I am. This is the community with which I am familiar and whose names are etched on stone in that Whitefield cemetery.

I need to know who has been preserved for another week, as well as who has been tragically and prematurely 'bowled out.' I can discover at a glance who has given birth, who has married, who has unfortunately fallen ill and who has thankfully recovered. I must establish which bar mitzvah or wedding I ***haven't*** been invited to yet again. It appears that I was not born to be a socialite, but not to worry. I don't do 'fall outs.' I will manage without their invitations.

This is the community of which I am an inescapable part, and yet not. If the person mentioned isn't related to me, they will very probably be related to someone else whom I know well. This is indicative of a little known fact, that there are relatively few Jewish people in this country. Indeed, as I mentioned earlier on in my journey, the whole world contains very few Jewish people at all. Numerically, we are surprisingly insignificant – comprising about 1% of the Christian population worldwide. There are 13 or so million Jews in the world of which approximately 280,000 live in Britain. These are minute figures and are to anyone not familiar with them a genuine revelation. I should also add, merely in passing, that most Jews live in Israel and New York, not that you probably need to know that.

This reminds me of a Jewish prayer that the late Jewish singer/songwriter Leonard Cohen adapted to a song, the title of which is: '*who by Fire'.* I am fond of the song, but do find the prayer from which it is extracted quite disturbing, as it refers to God apparently deciding who should die in the forthcoming year and, moreover, by what means. Not that pleasant a lyric really.

By fire, ***by water***, in the sunshine, in the night or in the day, the song alternates. I think this is where the phrase '*the fear of God'* must surely come from, as it sends a real shiver down my spine. Yet this forms the very backbone of Jewish belief at the New Year, and probably explains the reason for the sudden burst of enthusiasm for synagogue attendance at this particular time of year. Attendance figures soar through the shule roof. As evidence of this fear. Many regular non-attendees inevitably do everything they can to avoid an untimely death as they hedge their bets with the Almighty and show up for their annual pilgrimage. We cannot be blamed for this. Who really fancies the idea of ***death by fire***, or even ***strangulation*** - within the next twelve months? Definitely, not me. It sounds altogether ghastly. He has some very odd ideas, I fear.

When we are in synagogue, we can benefit from the chat, the odd prayer and a wink in the direction of the clouds. We are ever hopeful that God will reveal Himself to us just in time, by demonstrating benevolence regardless of the true extent of our last year's transgressions. We are weak and we succumb to the line of least resistance. We believe sometimes just in case. I am troubled by this supposed '***quid pro quo'*** theory and in my view the equally misconceived approach to prayer with a transparently selfish motive. If I die this year, I pray for mercy that it may at least be a painless death. This is similar to the image of the confession box on a Friday when the priest sits in judgment on his Catholic congregants. With utmost respect, I do find it all rather bizarre.

Am I to presume that those who died in the last twelve months were written in the big Black Book last New Year? It seems a particularly crude way of expressing an intimate relationship with our Creator, and only serves to confirm the notion of the selfish gene as expounded so cynically by Richard Dawkins, the devoutly Atheist author. I cannot pretend to be keen on this notion of doing deals with God, and I have my doubts as to whether they ever do truly occur. Were it to be like this, the lottery fund would be bankrupt and even eager Branson would not even consider a further bid. Every prayer would be automatically answered and everyone would inevitably believe in his or her God and Saviour. But, of course, the unfortunate corollary may be that God brought down a curse on the Jews with the advent of Fascism, and imposed upon my people the ultimate punishment for our assimilation. It is all just a little too simplistic for my liking.

I sometimes wonder why the One who creates us makes it so incredibly difficult for some of us to recognize Him. Why all this mystery? If He truly came down from Mount Sinai, would it be so terrible for Him to march down my particular road if only to reassure me that it wasn't all a pack of lies? Why all this mystery? Why, oh why? This is a theme to which I shall be returning later on as I journey along, when I shall plead with God to show his face to me. But that's a little later on.

Just as I had done in the cemetery on that bitter and crisp September day, I now dip carefully and poignantly into the obituary pages, reflecting on life's true meaning, perusing the list of names, stopping at familiar ones and trusting that I do not catch sight of my own obituary right now.

Death by Fire. I can think of nothing worse than this. I picture the scene at Kings Cross, and the screams of those helpless innocents in captivity. My mind wanders to the waters cascading down the decks of the Herald of Free Enterprise. I wonder what or who God actually is to allow such misery to ensue, whether by water or by fire, and whether as a result of human error or God's will. I feel as if I really do know nothing.

Blame human beings if you wish, my Lord, but you created them too. Without you, it was definitely not possible. You are omnipotent (or so I am told), and therefore I can only assume that you had the power to step in and stop this devastation. The tsunami and even the lesser floods as far afield as Gloucestershire and Rawalpindi, the earthquakes of India and

Haiti, the hurricanes in New Jersey, the typhoon in the Philippines, death by flood, by fire, by strangulation or by whatever, were all not surely possible without God's own creativity. The list and extent of human tragedy is almost infinite, as is the extent of human evil. Being Jewish – so where does that get me? How does my Jewishness help to explain to those victims what went wrong?

Had He not been responsible for creation, they would not be the victims. In my most philosophical moments, I can relax in the apparent knowledge that God is in fact the name for the blank page that I cannot otherwise fill. He is the personification of the mystery, to which I consistently and inevitably return. He is the answer when there is no other logical explanation at all. He is the goodness that we crave for. He is what goes beyond all parameters of logic and understanding

There again, it was God who surely instilled in us a propensity to do evil. I sometimes try to rationalize with Him, and I am sure I will do so many times again. It would have been so much easier if evil did not exist at all and would have been preferable just to have good and then perhaps, **very** good. I assume that it was in God's remit to merely create shades of goodness in which case evil would have been something we might fear, but never have to actually experience. Evil is a perfectly horrible state of being, and yet we are supposedly created in God's image. Were we evil or innocent at birth? I gather different religions have different answers. I have none. Because I know nothing. Or very little.

These fateful pages I refer to in the Jewish newspapers tell the tale of this Jewish community in its totality. It bares its soul for me to witness. It marks the beginning and the end, and the in-between for good measure. It reflects vibrant Jewish celebration, as it simultaneously mirrors communal mourning for every lost soul in its midst. It tells the story of the path and the progress of English Jews in all parts of the United Kingdom, its growth and its slide, its vitality and its despair. Its incline in numbers might be counterbalanced by its decline in religious fervour, or whichever way round is currently the case. The fact is that I still see many black hats and curls wherever I travel and Jewish life appears to be proliferating worldwide with religious Jews customarily aspiring to even larger families. And larger trilbies too. There is an upsurge of so-called **Charedi*** Jews who appear to me to be arguably rather extreme and potentially divisive, but who appear to be growing in number nevertheless. I hear all sorts of dastardly news. Inter-communal uprisings and some religious Jews behaving very badly. As my mum would say – it takes all sorts. But I was brought up to expect more from those who have genuine belief in Hashem.

The announcements page tells the story week-by-week, day-by-day, minute-by-minute of the circuitous journey of a section of the Jewish people in a particular Semitic community. The integration, the segregation, the degradation as the Jewish people journey on, documented in a weekly Jewish newspaper is the story of the comings and goings that are recorded for posterity. The story it tells is transparent. It also makes a clear and unequivocal statement, if only by inference, that Jewish life lives on. Despite all adversity, these pages celebrate the survival of the Jewish people. Each birth is a *re*birth of the Jewish race as an entity, a tribe, worthy of preservation. A Jewish newspaper, the kosher shops, the synagogue, Hebrew classes, Jewish charities; these are all hallmarks of a Jewish community and its fabric. They are the bricks with which the Jewish community is built. They represent its vital infrastructure.

As a Holocaust survivor finally reaches the end of his precious life, a baby is born in his honour and bears the grandfather's Hebrew name. This element of **Continuity** is one of the most significant driving forces of both religious and secular Jewish lives.

This is indicative of my own Jewish identity, as I can never truly be in total isolation as long as the Jewish people survive. We, the so-called Israelites, stoically march on undaunted through our personal wilderness, regardless of our own individual religious beliefs, however tenuous they may be.

In times of celebration and at times of personal tragedy, we Jews seemingly become a homogenous group once again as we pull together – more in unison than at any other time. We perished together, but we also survive together. Those with big black hats and with *payot,* * and with dutifully pasty faces mingle begrudgingly or not at a Jewish funeral with ladies in trousers and skirts above the knee. We pay similar respects in our own particular ways, but as one people. We have our differences but we remain one people, if only at times of personal and communal tragedy or celebration.

Jewish ritual is followed by all of us in a not dissimilar way. For those daunting moments, we are just Jews huddled together to comfort one another or to share times of elation. Whether with a Star of David on our obligatory armband or a *mezuzah*,* there are many things that inextricably bind us together. Often they are symbols, sometimes only thoughts, but we are destined to all be - the Wandering Jews. We are inevitably linked, if only because of our need to preserve our shared heritage.

I frequently sit alone in a quiet corner of the house on a Friday night poring over these obituaries in the Jewish papers in a slightly obsessive, but not morbid, way. They can be profoundly moving. As I read the words composed by a husband about his parted and cherished wife, I often shed a silent tear. I say aloud the words that refer to a departed son or daughter and shiver at the thought of such earth-shattering events. I mouth the words of such loss and utter devotion as I read that every mother, father, uncle, auntie, grandmother or grandfather have borne their illnesses with such '**remarkable dignity**', whilst every spouse seemingly was a '**best friend**' lost forever. I sometimes wonder to myself whether the survivors left it too late (just as I did with my great uncle Max) to express themselves personally by conveying such adoration to the deceased during their lifetime. I cannot help but reflect on the purpose of life itself just as I did when I began my journey in the cemetery grounds.

Jewish people regard ourselves as having lost one of our own, and we grieve communally and collectively for them in their moment of loss. We are one less Jew and we can feel their loss personally and profoundly. This is what a community is about, sharing the good times but also the bad. We are recognized for our innate sense of community, and we do habitually share the celebration and the grief together within our own small communities.

And at this time, I am bound to think of my father again who died all those many years ago, well before the Millennium was ever even contemplated. 1979 – an age ago, and yet only yesterday. He knew nothing of the Millennium Wheel - spinning round in its infinite orbit. I think of how upset he was when I didn't always kiss him on the cheek and I am angry with myself that I should ever have missed such a special opportunity to demonstrate the precious love of a child for a father. I was too young to understand then, but now it is much too late to make amends. I cannot re-live the chance my father once gave me when I was too immature to appreciate the uniqueness of a father's embrace. I had a father who was never unwell - until he was. Reduced to a thin stick of flesh on bones, he was destined to reduce me to tears, as I became fatherless at a stroke.

Too late, too late to ever say goodbye. It's far, far too late to ask the questions that will forever remain unanswered. Whether Jacob Fireman really **did** believe in God, having witnessed the skeletons at Bergen-Belsen, or whether, like me, he was hoping for a meaning to this disorder, but could never be absolutely certain. I know that my father wanted his children to believe, to have hope and if possible to have genuine faith. He wanted me to believe that there was a purpose to life, and that our *Maker* (as he put it so hesitantly) had an overall design for us. He wanted me to believe, more than he probably believed himself, just as I do with my own children. The very mention of Atheism was, to him, abhorrent - just as it is for me. *No God* equated to no *Hope* and an acceptance of the futility of it all. This was beyond the pale for him. He had to instil *Hope*, if nothing more. Belief amounted to *Hope* amounted to purpose and a semblance of good order. It had to be, as the alternative was too hard to bear. Even if it was illusory, as Dawkins claims, we had to go on hanging on to *Hope.* And I do.

There is a huge, gaping hole in our lives that people like me do not fully comprehend. Most of us are desperate to fill it with a kindly face, a long flowing beard and even a white kaftan. Even if we do not know the answers, it is probable He may. We dream. This is what I hope for, as I search for a purpose whilst striving to discover the answers that constantly elude me.

In my imagination, I am wandering once again in the same cemetery in sombre yet safe and familiar surroundings, overcome by its poignancy and the sheer pointlessness which engulf me like a whirlwind. Words on pages signify euphoria or devastation, merely with a turn of a single phrase, or the juxtaposition of two single words. The desolation is palpable.

Almost every local Jewish death is recorded in these weekly announcement columns alongside the births, the marriages, the bar mitzvahs, the unveilings (*the tomb settings*) and all other similar staging posts on a Jewish life's ethnic journey. They tell the developing tale of Jewish communal life, just as the cemetery does.

On these pages, the future of the Jewish people is determined, as one life is cruelly extinguished whilst another bursts forth ecstatically from the womb. These pages are where life and death sit uncomfortably and incongruously side by side as rather uneasy bedfellows. But unlike the cemetery where death is the victor, here there is a welcome balance between hopelessness and *Hope*, the end and a new beginning, the laughter as well as the tears. These weekly announcements express condolences on the one hand and congratulations on the other and yet, taken in the round, they tell the whole unscripted story. It is a diary of mixed emotions, comprising the tragic and the euphoric ups and downs of a closely-knit community that goes on wandering. They express the random nature of life itself.

This is where a single and unique Jewish life begins and ends, and where Jewish rituals mark out each precious life and death. These are the very same people I once knew and who are part of my extended family.

The life cycle is enacted on these pages and I am moved, just as I was in the cemetery on that serenely sunny September day.

Life's journey is crumbling before my very eyes as it defines itself, if only by its fragility and its intrinsic and inevitable mortality. God hides behind the wispy clouds and taunts and teases me in a weary way. He tells me nothing, and yet He teaches me everything I know.

The curious word that Jews customarily use at all these various occasions good and bad is: '*lechayim**' simply translated: '*to life.*'
It is the same word that is uttered and spluttered when we drink wine and other alcoholic beverages, and which typifies a zest for and a real appreciation of life itself. But even at a funeral or at a shiva house, the greeting of consolation is one that relies upon hope. We say to one another: 'long life'. When the period of mourning is over, we have a ***kiddush**** when we drink wine and wish one another a lechayim, a wish for a long life yet again. At funerals and shiva houses, we do not necessarily dress in black, but nor are there any flowers. But we celebrate life itself. ***To Life.***

Life, to life, to a precious life, a positive sentiment signifying the value we place on every single, solitary life. Even if we are not certain where God is, we have to respect a human life in all its majesty and glory. In English we might say '*life goes on'* in a rather nonchalant if not an almost negative way, as we reflect upon the inevitable. The Jewish custom is to look to the future, and to value not just the life that has just ended, but the life that is unbreakable. To celebrate the continuity of life amongst men and, more particularly, the continuity of the Israelites.

And so in Jewish talk, we say on every conceivable occasion: 'lechayim' - to life. Even at times of real sadness, we reach out for the sign of rebirth, hope and we exclaim - lechayim – to life. If you ever had the good fortune to see Fiddler on the Roof at the theatre or on film, you will recall the celebratory song: 'To Life, To Life, lechayim' It was sung against the background of the pogroms in Eastern Europe at the time. One of Tevye's daughters is marrying Motel the tailor and they drink to life - lechayim. We Jews are taught to appreciate the gift of life as a positive message and a reminder of our own survival. In Jewish law, each life is precious, whether a Jewish one or not. What greater gift than life itself? Any life, regardless of which religion. Every life has a priceless value, well beyond mere words.

In the course of my journey, I have begun to realize that the mystery of life is life itself - the question as to how we are created, and for what eventual purpose. The miracle of life is life itself, its mystery and its wonders. I am not certain exactly what I mean by a *miracle,* and yet I know that Life itself is the perfect embodiment of such a concept. I have marvelled at the sight of childbirth, and then the growth from babyhood to adulthood. A little babbling, titchy thing grows over the course of time into a lanky, articulate adult who learns to answer back. We often take this all for granted - until something untoward happens. Yet life itself is the miracle that we all witness every single day. It is here for all to see. Life breathes. Nature blossoms. The trees grow and then shed their leaves with the change of the seasons. Light and darkness replace one another in a timely fashion. The sun shines from time to time. This is magical, if not positively miraculous.

I now start to accept that trite explanations as to how we arrived on this earth will never satisfy me. This is the eternal mystery and I need not necessarily look further. The miracle has fallen in our lap - within the confines of our own lifetime, and stares at us knowingly. We call it nature. **And nature is the miracle. Explain nature without a creator, and I may have to believe an alternative version. But not yet.**

In Jewish ritual and practice, at times of great elation and similarly at times of deep sorrow, the Jewish community is at its very zenith. On these occasions our differences can be sidestepped, however fleetingly, in order that we may share the moment together. Proudly standing shoulder to shoulder as one people, we finally appear to grasp the vital but sometimes prickly nettle. This sense of community is real and intense. We are willing to become public property again, and the wanderers return as we walk briskly and resolutely together in order to bury a member of our community or, much better still, celebrate a wedding of two of our own. Like the young Jewish girls in their trailing black raincoats who cover any trace of residual flesh, we walk together in unison. We share in one another's grief, just as we celebrate each other's happiness. To each, there is a lechayim and to everyone there is a desire to celebrate 'only simchas.'

The alternative is what befell my great uncle Max – a death in pathetic and unwarranted isolation. This empathy at times of great moment makes Jewish life very special. What I visualize on these occasions is the lone wanderer returning home again. I, in particular, return to the community of which I am forever part and from whom I may be distanced, but from whom I never wish to be entirely divorced. This is who I am. Black hats, grey hats or no hats at all – these are my people, all interpreting their Judaism in their own personal way, but all Jews nevertheless.

Should I ever wish to do so, I will never be able to set myself free, if only because Jewish identity is an inseparable part of who I am. My

Jewishness runs through my veins like seaside rock. It defines who I am, what I am and the values I believe in. It is like a limb, a part of what makes me the person I am.

For me, these are the occasions that are *spiritually* uplifting, and where life's daily challenges are subrogated, as we journey onto to a higher spiritual plain. For me, this can often represent Jewish life at its most generous and satisfying. For each occasion, there are a multitude of customs, rituals and religious laws that reflect the value placed upon the dignity of a single human life by the Jewish religion. I may have a series of issues with some of the minutiae, but I would never seek to argue with the basic premise that life is a gift to be treasured and celebrated.

And so it is that every Jew needs to cry out for peace, and deplore with moral courage and outrage the loss of one single life in war. War is awful and every single death tragic. The repeated newsreel of Wootton Bassett and its line of wooden caskets carrying dead soldiers was once testament to the real losers in the past wars in Iraq and Afghanistan. War is real. War is cruel.

If I were ever to discover God in His full munificence, it would inevitably be at a time when I see a healthy child born. But I cannot overlook the fact that the opposite must be equally true. I consider the devastation that cannot be ameliorated by words of comfort, when another innocent, newly born child starts their life's journey in ill health. I cannot help but wonder where God was on *that* day. He has no answers for me. It is He who has caused the suffering to those parents and I have no idea why. This is part of the mystery too. I owe the baby's parents the obligation to ask why. And I do.

When I was young I knew the answers and yet so many years later, I feel as if I know nothing. Indeed, the only thing I seem to truly know is that I know so very little. Upon reflection, I think that this may well be the definition of maturity, the point at which I first appreciated that I actually knew almost nothing. Once upon a time I accepted what I saw at face value and what I heard as reliable, and yet years later I believe so little, whether it is politicians screwing the public by dishonestly over-claiming their expenses, or the clergy denouncing other segments of our society whilst abusing the vulnerable. There are many challenges and endless injustices and it is intrinsically unfair to ignore them.

As to 'miracles', I am not certain exactly what I mean, but I am willing to concede that the birth of a child is self-evidently and indisputably miraculous. The heart beating in the womb, the limbs programmed to work relentlessly for a lifetime, the eye that sees, the hand that touches, the nose that smells, the ear that hears. These faculties and senses are wondrous by reference to any human benchmark, and Darwin cannot for me personally explain their true evolutionary process. These are an integral part of that special miracle, and it is right and proper that I respect the life that has been created for whatever real purpose there may be.

The law of evolution can never answer for me what was at the beginning of time, and who or what was the initial creator or creative force. God represents the unexplained, the faith, the mystery and most of all the ***Hope***. Without the faintest hope of a creative force, there is no order and no purpose. We all must struggle for direction in order to seek out relevant answers to these fundamental questions.

As the tiny baby cried, I yelled out with uncontrollable and overpowering joy. This was the precise moment that was incomparable to anything else I had previously experienced, particularly its intensity and my resultant indescribable relief. I cried spontaneously, totally oblivious to anyone else in that delivery room whom I might offend. This was our selfish moment and ecstasy oozed out of every pore of my body. The knife went in and out came a breathing bundle with a beating heart, a shrill and welcoming cry, predictably wrinkled, but very much alive. A new life had begun its journey just like mine and my little baby had inhaled breath into her tiny lungs. I witnessed a miracle that day, one that I will never forget or take for granted. I saw it with my own eyes. Even an Apple Mac couldn't create something as incredible as this.

At that exact time, I felt that I had cheated God by ever daring to doubt Him and his boundless skill in creating Life. Yet my hypocrisy is brazen, because almost as soon as the moment passes, doubts start to return. Babies with disabilities, mothers without children, wives without husbands, babies without parents. This is a cruel and harsh truth that I cannot overlook in my own moments of personal ecstasy.

Who do ***they*** have to thank for ***their*** grief? Where is ***their*** God? But without any faith, we don't get off first base. Faith alone answers the unanswerable, helping to fill the gaping hole with meaning and purpose. I feel the need to thank someone for what has happened to us at this particular time. I need to demonstrate my gratitude, not just to the doctors who helped the embryo reach the end of her sticky journey, but to thank the Creator who enabled the journey to be embarked upon at all. For these few seconds, I recreate the image of this kindly King on his throne sprinkling silver dust upon us as our fairy tale comes to a glorious fruition. I am in dreamland, detached from the troubled world.

I go on sobbing for what feels like an eternity. I cannot believe my good fortune as I hear the cry of our newly born child and I desperately and instinctively look upwards towards the sky to express my gratitude. I talk of ***Hope*** and ***faith*** and I wonder endlessly which one of the two comes first. Does ***hope*** precede faith - or does faith instil hope? I reflect upon our other daughters too, Vikki and Louise, and our gorgeous grandchildren making their way through life, and cannot help but marvel at the miracle of birth and then the passage through life as they all grow up too quickly, as we all do.

I am now clear entirely clear that I never want to lose the ***Hope***, though blind faith presently eludes me. Only at certain times does my optimism spill over into some kind of genuine faith, as on the occasion which I have just described, the birth of a new, breathing, unique life. The creation of a child on earth capable of such immense achievement is bound to be a source of unrestricted joy.

It was in Genesis that God commanded Man to:

……….***'Be fruitful and multiply.'***

It appears to be a simple enough commandment. The implication is that we should produce as many children as humanly possible in order to fulfil this commandment. However, I now gather that the ***Talmud**** dictates that it is only necessary to produce one son and one daughter in order to follow this command.

In the Eastern European villages, the Jews seemed to have large families, as did many first generation immigrant Jews to England. Religious Jews nowadays appear to push a fine array of designer prams, and there is great celebration in having large families. This may, I assume, have more to do with contraception than purely fulfilling dreams. But the custom among religious Jews is to have large families and to fulfil the greatest possible ***mitzvah****. Though the pain of childbirth is reputedly a punishment from God for Eve's transgressions, Judaism has always considered children to be a gift from God. There is little doubt that family life and the love of children are at the very forefront of traditional Jewish life.

Before the child is born, and in the first three days after the birth, the mother's health is regarded as a priority. In Jewish law, I have already made clear that each life is regarded as of unique value. Within our close communities, each birth of a Jewish child is as I have also mentioned, a communal birth, and therefore a time of shared celebration. In the diaspora, Jews give the newly born child a conventional name for daily use, but also a Hebrew name for religious purposes. Currently, biblical names are acceptable in everyday use, and the two often converge as, for example, with Joshua or Jacob. What is more moving is the custom to name a Jewish new born in a manner intended to preserve the Jewish heritage. It is the Hebrew name that is used when called to read from the Torah, when marrying under the chuppah, and when we are buried. To whatever extent we choose to assimilate, we return to our roots at these momentous times. Yet again the theme of the Wandering Jew is revitalised.

In Hebrew, our name is always expressed as 'A'- son or daughter of - 'B'. This epitomizes the continuity of the Jewish people. Similarly, we do not acquire the name of a living parent, but rather of a relative who has died, thereby perpetuating their memory and celebrating the lifecycle of the Jewish people as a whole. This once again is an aspect of our continuity, befitting a people so nearly wiped out at the hand of evil on so many dreadful occasions throughout history

The birth of a Jewish child is a matter of enormous pride and communal euphoria. Despite assimilation, the Jewish People live on and each and every birth celebrates that continuity. It is analogous to passing on the cherished baton in a relay race. I definitely regard myself as having an obligation **not to let the team down**. This is what I referred to earlier as **Continuity**. There is, as a result of immense suffering over the centuries, an insatiable need in me to ensure that the Jewish people survive, if only to go on telling the story of the Exodus from Egypt and all the atrocities that have befallen us. That we can sit round a Seder table at Pesach and repeatedly answer our children's questions again and again.

It is what *Tevye* called: *tradition*. This means an awful lot to me. It is clear that I have this unflinching need to preserve the Jewish way of life, its culture and its customs. I feel compelled to ensure that the Jews who perished in the gas chambers of the concentration camps are remembered, their values and their bravery preserved forever. I feel as if I have a duty as a Wandering Jew to go on preserving that story.

Whilst the outside world is rapidly changing on a daily basis, often transformed beyond recognition, Jewish traditions often harking back to my childhood symbolize this continuity and longevity. They remain substantially intact and represent a welcome relief and simplicity. These are rituals that remind me of another era when life was far less complicated, and much more straightforward. They represent stability and a decent set of values. Our culture survives throughout each decade whilst all around us changes. It is Jewish traditional life that is the constant, defined by its calmness and communal spirit, and this is an important part of its intrinsic value.

In England, a day of rest might be a thing of the past, but in the Orthodox Jewish faith, it represents an opportunity to switch off the i-pad and the mobile phone, ignore news of political strife and take a break from life's incessant stresses. It has some self-evident benefits for those willing to make those sacrifices.

It is obvious to me that from the moment of conception, should we choose to be part of our inherited Jewish world, we are defined by that Jewishness. I am part of a wandering people with whom I am inescapably connected, and who have rules and customs and a long and distinguished heritage. We are a clan, a tribe, and most of all, a community.

In the eyes of Jewish law, the newly born child is born without sin, though personally I have grave doubts about this. We enthusiastically celebrate the baby's safe arrival as living proof of God's work, as well as the survival of the Jewish people against all odds. The often-remote link to our religion shines through the darkest clouds.

I cannot of course be sure that Jewish law places any more emphasis upon the value of a single life than any other religion, but what I do know is that my own Jewish background and upbringing have had a significant effect upon the way I view each single life.

It is also hardly surprising that the Jewish religion has something fundamental to say about abortion too, the early termination of a single and precious life. It would be odd if Judaism regarded abortion with any element of indifference, and this is certainly not the case. Though, unlike Catholicism, Jews do not regard life as being extant once there is an embryo, abortion is certainly not encouraged. If, however, the mother's life is at risk, her life must be protected and preserved wherever possible. The Jewish faith does not put the liberty and the rights of the mother before the embryo, in so far as it does not promote the woman's right to terminate the birth, merely because she is free to do so. Each life, both child and parent, is of immense value. I feel compassion for the woman who is traumatized at this time, just as I do for the child who has no voice. I have never walked in the woman's shoes and so the line between *yes* and ***no*** remains indistinct.

Circumcision is a significant emblem and celebration of pure Jewishness. It is a longstanding ritual in the Jewish faith that a newly born boy is circumcised, eight days after his birth. It can and must indeed be performed on the Sabbath or even on Yom Kippur if that day falls accordingly. There are so many rules and regulations applicable to the circumcision performed by the mohel, most of which I do not know. The person who merely holds the baby whilst the ceremony is performed is greatly honoured in fulfilling that role; there is a blessing, and the relatives and friends who are invited to witness the circumcision bless the child. It is a very tearful, but at the same time an immensely happy, occasion, and symptomatic of the longevity of this particular Jewish ritual. Like the mezuzah, the **brit** makes another unequivocal statement that the survival of the Jewish people shall be celebrated. It is a pronouncement that we make, as a constant reminder of who we are. Yet again we return to that recurring theme of **Continuity** that is so significant to me, if only because these rituals have survived for millennia. There had to be a reason.

I do not thankfully remember my own circumcision, but I can certainly vouch for the fact that it took place, as I bear the scars. I presumably cried like all the other tiny Jewish babies have done over the centuries. Since then, I have attended quite a few such occasions. Rather like Jewish weddings, these are the times when my Jewishness runs through my heart and soul. Despite the scream of the little baby, and the understandable distress of the mother and father, these are the customs that I cannot help but cling on to. If anything symbolizes **Continuity**, then this highly charged ritual is it.

These traditions are an essential part of who I am. This is an integral element of my heritage and the history of my people that inevitably brings us together again as a community. But this ritual, that is not unique to Jews but also for example practiced in the Moslem faith, is quintessentially Jewish. It is a sign that we are who we are, different, proud and survivors. Jewish boys from all backgrounds are marked for life, and identified as Jews for a lifetime. This is a Jewish mark of enormous significance in fulfilling our promise of Jewish **Continuity**. Whilst only a small proportion of Jewish men will wear a yarmulke in their everyday life, most Jewish men religious or not will have been 'scarred'. Similarly, there is a mezuzah on the door of most Jewish houses, and a Star of David is often worn around the neck. To varying extents, we choose to identify ourselves and to set ourselves apart. Some are less overt, there will be those who are ashamed of who they are, but most Jews I know are happy to declare their Jewishness with pride. We don't necessarily have to flaunt it but nor do we need to hold our heads in shame. We have learned to answer back.

It is true that when anti-Semitism has thrived, it has often been accompanied by a prohibition on circumcision. For religious Jews, it marks the covenant between God and Abraham. For me, the Wandering Jew, it signifies a new Jewish birth according to Jewish ritual and, in a symbolic way, the survival of the Jewish people. It demonstrably signifies our amazing ability to survive, despite incessant and ruthless persecution. It represents communal celebration in the face of continuing anti-Semitism in many parts of the world. Most graphically, it spits on Hitler's grave.

For me as I have said, it is about the ***Continuity*** of a faith – yes, but also of a culture, a race and a people. To hurt a child like this at such a tender age whilst his mother is so distraught is, on a certain level, sheer madness. It is a seemingly archaic ritual that borders on the barbaric. For this reason, it is under threat in certain parts of Europe. And yet the Wanderer returns to his roots as I hear the scream of the child, witness the family around him and honour a sacred custom that has been practiced and preserved from time immemorial. It is a ritual that lives on, just like the people who adhere to the practice. Community. Continuity. Custom.

I just cannot help it – it makes me feel (perhaps for all the wrong reasons) rejuvenated. It is a true celebration, and one of which I am ultimately happy to be a part, despite any niggling doubts I may have about paining a baby so young and defenceless.

I stand stoically witnessing a ceremony that has survived. The child screams, the mother yells, and I cry yet more tears of happiness. Other religions may have circumcisions but, as far as I am aware, only Jews relish this special ritual as a symbol of survival. The baby is a Jewish baby and the baby must scream. It is a shrill sound, one like the shofar sounded at our New Year. It is a very moving ceremony, and a recognised and respected facet of Jewish life.

I cannot help but be in awe at God's greatest miracle and it is at these moments of elation that I become embroiled in my own neurological machinations.

Is there – isn't there? Who I am? Why am I drawn to this religion of which I actually know so little? Why am I proud to be part of a seemingly cruel ritual with arguable medical benefit, but great religious significance? What do I actually believe?

I must now take a circuitous detour to Birkenau. I have travelled to the camps at Auschwitz on three separate occasions. On each occasion, there was a terrible feeling of emptiness as I walked along the old train lines, adjacent to the endless rows of battered but partially preserved barracks. I had to imagine the intense suffering, and I felt drained. Stone stairs lead down to a desolate room where the Zyklon B gas was once pumped into a confined chamber, and from where heaps of corpses were gratuitously removed (often by other helpless inmates). I saw it all, and I remained silent and dazed.

But it was when Rabbi Barry Marcus, who led my first visit, recited the ***kaddish*** * that I became hysterical and totally out of control. I wept for those helpless souls. As I did so, I tried to hide in a corner through embarrassment until the rabbi came over to me, took me in his arms and let me cry and whimper until I had no tears left, my eyes were too sore and my tear ducts were empty. It was as if I had vomited; I was drained of energy and silently exhausted.

Just as I had collapsed in a heap when I had seen Alfie Bass many years earlier, here I was, at the actual site of those most horrendous events in history, bereft, hysterical and comforted by a compassionate rabbi who understood me. He knew why I was crying and had probably comforted many other helpless Jews like me before. I felt helpless. My tears meant nothing.

Those words of Hebrew I had heard recited were words with which I was familiar, and they reminded me once more of the history of the Jewish people. The majority of those innocent victims who had perished so needlessly were Jewish. They had no choice - and nor do I. We are born to be Jewish. This is who we are. This is who I am. I cried for all those of any faith who were so callously abused and obliterated by the sadistic Nazi regime.

But it was a Jewish prayer that finally struck me down. This was the memorial prayer for six million human beings wiped out with vicious and callous impunity. This is the kaddish prayer, the same memorial prayer we recite for every deceased Jew whether a prince or a pauper, religious or secular, male or female, young or old. This is a universal Jewish prayer for the dead, and was recited this day with enormous sadness at the concentration camp where the inmates had been promised that their work would buy them their freedom and which turned out to be a cruel and heartless lie. I was utterly distraught. There were no birds flying over this horrendous memorial to innocent men, women and children. Even ***they*** flew off to another place, where the stench of desecrated bodies, and the memory of death wasn't in the air. This was like Whitefield cemetery - but a million times worse. This was witnessing not just death. In Auschwitz, I was the witness to murder.

I was helpless. My tears meant nothing. I was too late to help.

It is hardly any wonder that Jews take pride in a Jewish birth, and defeating the Nazis and Fascism wherever they raise their vile and ugly heads. It is also not surprising that I should emphasize the **Continuity** of the Jewish people as being at the very root of who I am, and what I do. It is right and proper that I spend every day of my life preaching tolerance and deploring all forms of racism. This is the duty of a Jew. This is my duty.

Because: ***If not me, who?***

The Holocaust has had a massive impact upon me. Thank goodness for Jewish weddings which are momentous occasions, celebrating not just the union between a bride and groom, but also the future of our people. I value the longevity of our rituals and customs of which there are so many, closely associated with the wedding ceremony itself.

When I think of a wedding, I can see the chuppah, the bride encircling her groom, the ceremonial smashing of the glass, the boisterous exclamations of ***mazel tov*** * and the dancing with the bride and groom both hoisted onto chairs held aloft by their friends. All these aspects of a wedding ceremony are indicative of the way Jews celebrate a marriage, with great exuberance, emotion, reflection and commitment. And with community.

Jewish weddings are for me exceedingly special as they once again represent an important element of my Jewish identity. They represent **Continuity** and survival. We return at these times to who we were born to be. The catering is generally kosher, and we dance separately, men with men, and women with women. We have this strange yearning on these special occasions to return to our roots. The Wandering Jews return to a simpler, uncomplicated, innocent time when Jews lived in their villages and cared for one another. There is a certain comfort in returning to a previous era. We do what frum Jews do, and at these times pretend that life has not changed. On days like this, we return.

All weddings, whatever their nature or religious identity, can be wonderful occasions. They signify a commitment by one human being to another for life. It is the playing out of the love story. I am not suggesting that Jews do it any better than Christians, Greek Orthodox or those of the Moslem faith, but we just do it differently, and in our own distinctive and singular way. It is these differences that make it all so extraordinary to a Jewish person like me. It is the traditions that have been passed on from generation to generation that I find inspiring. It is yet again the recurring theme of **Continuity** about which the former Chief Rabbi Jonathan Sacks himself has spoken so many times. The Jews are the wanderers, the

Israelites and, thankfully, the survivors. These customs and rituals are defined as Jewish. The bride is visited by her groom before the actual ceremony. The immediate families wait patiently under the chuppah for the arrival of the bride and her father (or the person giving her away), and then the short but moving ceremony commences with huge anticipation. It is a service spoken partially in Hebrew and enhanced by piercing Jewish melodies sung by the *chazzan** The bride encircles her groom seven times, a cup of wine is passed from one family member to another under the flower clad canopy and each person drinks from the same cup. The rabbi reads from the **Ketubah***. It is one of those occasions when ecstasy is again in abundance. It is a truly memorable occasion, the format of which has remained largely unchanged for centuries.

And the moment arrives, as depicted in many Hollywood tearjerkers, when a glass held in a protective sack is placed on the marble floor under the canopy. There is a moment's hesitation. There is total momentary silence. And then the groom ceremoniously stamps on it. As the glass smashes, I think of **kristallnacht*** when the Nazis went on the rampage, smashing the windows of Jewish owned or occupied premises as a foretaste of what was about to be unleashed upon the Jewish population. Simultaneous with the breaking glass, the entire shule erupts into a wild frenzy of 'mazel tov.' The whole congregation is a vital part of this unique moment in time, epitomizing Jewish life in all its various guises, as we celebrate the future but simultaneously, in hearing the glass being smashed on the ground, we remember and respect the past. We think back over a troubled past and of those who have not survived. Most of all, we acknowledge the union between two Jewish partners playing their own part in securing the future survival of the whole Jewish nation, whilst the glass tempers the joy by reminding us of our own fragility. It is a unique ceremony with profound and spiritual impact. This is the communal recognition of the survival and hopefully, the rejuvenation of the Jewish people.

During these life-changing celebrations, even I am frum again - like the young man I once was when I was fussed over at shule with the havdalah candle, grasped in my clenched fist. I feed off the grandeur and the solemnity of the synagogue's atmosphere, and it is at these times that this particular wanderer returns to his religion, and to his roots and his community. This is who I am, and as I journey along, I realise the fact is that I just can't get away.

I desert the synagogue on the Sabbath, or even on Yom tov but I expect it to be there to marry my daughters. I am a Jew and sometimes, though rarely, a religious Jew. On these special occasions, God peers down through the grandiose, multi-coloured stained glass windows that adorn the synagogue and smiles on my family. I am dreaming and at these moments, as I see my daughter standing under that canopy with her new husband in the most traditionally Jewish way, I become a believer – just like dad would have always wanted. Suddenly I am walking along Bury New Road with a huge hat, curly locks and a siddur under my arm. Well, almost.

My *Hope* and my elation are bordering on faith as the glass smashes onto the tiles, and delighted relatives and friends scream out for joy. We want it to work out well for the new couple, and not just for them but for the entire Jewish people. We do not want Jewish life to be over right now. Sometimes onerous, it is immensely joyous and fulfilling as well.

And so this is who I am. I may wander off on a frolic of my own, but I inevitably return to my roots, to the songs I heard sung as a child, to my people, to memories of our suffering, and our incredible survival. I picture Israel battling against its encircling, pugnacious neighbours. I imagine Jews under constant threat from Fascists and racists, and I cannot help feeling a sense of fraternity and belonging. We are compelled to defend ourselves. I remember very well, when still a youngster, during the time of the Yom Kippur War in 1967, being on the edge of my stool in the kitchen at home as I listened nervously to the radio. I was wondering where it was all leading for both Israel and for Jews worldwide. It was terrifying as I contemplated what losing that war would truly mean to me.

When the catastrophic earthquake struck in Haiti in January 2010, mowing down several thousands of innocent adults and children in an already poverty-stricken country, I received an email from a Jewish friend in New York. Ben's message said that I should be aware that the Israeli Defence Force was first in to deal with the rescue mission, 220 personnel had landed there, and set up a field hospital. 'Zaka*' were there too as they are sadly experienced in identifying the dead. I am moved by their humanitarian actions, but I am not surprised. I feel proud when Ben tells me all this, and it reminds me of Magen David Adom*, the Israeli Ambulance service that, as I mentioned earlier, always appears on the scene after a terrorist atrocity in Israel.

As well as celebrating the happy occasions together, we can generally rely upon some support from our co-religionists when we are afflicted with illness or family bereavement. I would not have liked my father to have died without the shiva, that period of communal mourning.

And so a Jewish life, like any life, comprises the usual staging posts - birth, marriage, death, and the various occasions in between. But it is the particular customs that Jews follow that identify who I am. It is at these times that even irreligious and secular Jews return to their roots. We might wander away, but most of us wander back. It is these very rituals, however archaic or irrelevant they may appear to be, that often preserve the communal spirit of togetherness.

I am steeped in tradition – the customs, the tunes, the ethos, the culture. This is who I am. This particular Wandering Jew willingly returns - because this is where I belong. The traditions and the customs have become part of who I am and, though sometimes I may be chained to them against my will, most of the time I would not want these ancient rituals to be binned forever, as they play their special part in identifying who I am.

The traditions, customs and the rituals of the Jewish people are the territory with which I am familiar, and where I feel comfortable. I might seek to move away, but their spiritual magnetism draws me back to where I feel a sense of belonging. I am Jewish and, however far I may stray, I am who I am, and not what I always would like to be, nor who I think I might be. I am just who I am. Something intangible, ill-defined, anachronistic, lurks within my inner being.

I was born to be Jewish. And so I am. But the question still remains to be answered: what does 'Being Jewish' really, actually, truly mean? And thus, my personal journey continues, as I search for yet further answers to so many unanswered questions. This is a journey of discovery after all, and not merely 'a walk in the park.' I have gathered, as I have journeyed, that answers need to be discovered and don't automatically come knocking on my door.

And, therefore, my journey in search of my own personal Jewish identity continues.

- **CHAREDI** are a section of ultra Orthodox Jews and, to the best of my knowledge, the most secluded.

- **PAYOT** are the side locks of religious Jewish men.

- **MEZUZAH** means literally a doorpost but, in practice, refers to an encased portion of the Torah affixed to most of the internal and the external doors of a Jewish home.

- **LECHAYIM,** as you now already know, means 'To Life' and is often accompanied by lifting of the wine cup.

- **TALMUD** is the source from which the code of Jewish law is derived. It is made up of the Mishnah and the Gemara.

- **MITZVAH** means a good deed, performed in accordance with religious duty. It literally means 'commandment.'

- **BRIT MILA** refers to the covenant of circumcision.

- **KADDISH** is the memorial prayer, but in reality is a hymn of praises to God found in the Jewish prayer service.

- **MAZELTOV** is the well-known phrase meaning 'good luck' at a time of celebration.

- **KETUBAH** is, in reality, a type of pre-nuptial agreement, and an integral part of a Jewish marriage outlining the rights and responsibilities of the groom in relation to the bride.

- **KRISTALLNACHT** is the night of the broken glass, and more particularly representing the shattered storefront window of Jewish owned shops.

- **MAGEN DAVID ADOM** is Israel's national emergency medical, disaster ambulance service, literally meaning the 'Red star of David.'

CHAPTER EIGHT

THE 'TOO JEWISH' JEW

"I once wanted to become an Atheist but I gave up……they have no holidays"
HENRY YOUNGMAN

Only having embarked upon this soul-searching journey of self-discovery, did I start to truly appreciate how my life has been materially affected, at every twist and turn, by my own Jewish identity. This is true, not merely at times of birth, marriage and death, but probably every day of my life. For someone like me who professes a rather uncertain, if not a positively wavering, religious belief, I now realize how immersed I nevertheless am in Jewish ritual and custom. I am, it appears, a participant in the preservation and promotion of an archaic religion and culture, regardless of what is actually means to me, or what I truly believe.

It helps to define who I am, and it also provides certain boundaries that I now accept are pretty crucial in setting out 'my own stall'. Being Jewish is an important part of my life and the way I choose to live it. It impacts upon what I do, with whom I do, whom I marry, what I eat, and even **when** I eat whatever it is that I eat. It affects what I laugh at, as well as what makes me cry. I am engulfed by it, like a storm out of control. Though born and brought up in England, I still sometimes look in, as if from the side line, the child of Jewish immigrant grandparents.

Whether I actually make a conscience decision to be immersed in this way or whether it is just inevitable, I cannot be sure. This is presumably why I felt it necessary to ever contemplate embarking upon this particular journey at all. I don't know whether this emanates from a sense of pride, or whether I am, as I sometimes fear, the eternal Jewish Apologist. I might just be *too* Jewish, after all.

I am, it is now clear, full of contradictions, as Dalia in particular forever reminds me. But I tell her that, unless I adopt an extreme position, either of absolute Atheism or strict Orthodoxy, I am forever destined to be the hypocrite she seems to deplore. We are either fundamentalists or moderates, and I am in no doubt which option I prefer. I cannot see myself scoffing on a ham sandwich but, similarly, I do not picture myself donning a huge fur trimmed black hat either. I occupy the middle ground, though I have never been entirely certain exactly where in the middle I may be. Sometimes I am *too* Jewish, but at other times I may be not Jewish enough. I appear to pick and choose in a random way. I saw a Jewish chap only the other day who was wandering along the main road, minding his own business, wearing white tights, and a fur hat so huge that it must surely have hurt his head. I react spontaneously with open-mouthed disbelief, though not obvious enough to let him see. I start to think that I have just witnessed an apparition. This goes to the root of my ambivalence. Proud of *who* I am, ashamed of *what* I am; strip that away, and what do I have?

It is this particular conflict of ideas that has driven me to ask all of these questions following that fateful visit to a desolate cemetery, near leafy Philips Park. I argue the case for moderation, but appreciate that this is another form of hypocrisy as well. Maybe I just want the best of all worlds, and want to be Jewish, but not *too* Jewish. I want to be different, but not totally. I want to be separate, but not behind barbed wire. I want to integrate, but not to assimilate. I want to mock my own people, and yet I want to be part of them. I am on the periphery and yet I am firmly and undeniably right in the midst of it all. The indisputable fact is that I am in a state of unknowing. The more I search, the more questions are thrown up in my path. I jump in when it suits me, and then opt out when I choose, as if I am on a bouncy castle, bobbing around chaotically and erratically. As I have already described, I go past some nearby **shules** with indifference or abandon but then, in almost the very next moment, I go to enormous trouble to find other synagogues in faraway places. It's odd. I salute Israel's bravery and tenacity, yet I am critical of its apparent intransigence. The truth is that I am in a quandary, wondering where I stand, just as I have often wondered who I really am, and what the ultimate purpose is. I am the Jew who wanders from concept to concept, idea to idea. I am the archetypal Wandering Jew.

Kosher food, as with all things Jewish, is not without its own set of rules and contradictions. There are many culinary laws, the majority of which I probably don't even know. I am familiar with the basics, though the reasons that lie behind the rules are much less clear to me. There are certain meats we Jews cannot eat, with bacon and pork both being distinctly off the menu. Milk and meat products are not to be mixed, or even eaten consecutively without waiting for a defined period of time. We have separate dishes and utensils for milk and meat too. All manner of shellfish are disallowed, whilst we are permitted to eat most white fish, as long as they have both fins and scales. Our ritual slaughter of animals must always be supervised by a rabbi. There is a real mixed bag of rules and regulations that some Jews adhere to, whilst many others ignore, regarding them as irrelevant and out-dated. Some eat kosher food in the home, but eat non-kosher food when they are out and about. There are all possible combinations, as every Jew seeks to justify our own interpretation of Jewish life, and the most appropriate level of religious observance. For those who take a very strict view, they will have separate sinks, and more than one dishwasher in order to keep milk well away from meat. Strict religious observance can be an expensive business. I sometimes think to myself – what is this all for? What has this to do with belief in God? Even if one believes in God, does one have to adhere to these ancient edicts?

This is never more apparent than at Pesach, the festival of Passover, when we celebrate our exodus from Egypt, and our wandering in the wilderness for forty long, arduous years. We eat **_matzo,_*** unleavened bread - but not bread as we know it, and all food must pass the **_chametz_*** test. This additional supervision does not come cheap either. There are many who quite persuasively suggest that it is well of hand, and the food industries and retailers are taking full advantage of this annual Jewish festival, and its almost captive audience. To some Jews, it is just too commercialized, whilst to others it is an integral part of our Jewish faith. On certain days, when I may be feeling slightly more cynical, even I myself regard it all as a form of voodoo that has gone off the rails. Every year, there appears to be another food either banned or accepted by the **_Beth Din_***(the Jewish Rabbinical Court), interpreting our regulations as they seem to randomly choose to do. One year, Polo mints are kosher, the next year they aren't. Bottles of coke with a label, and consequently almost double the price, are suddenly 'kosher for Passover.' Is this what my God really wants me to do, to look at labels, and to pay double the price? Is this the choice he had in mind when he said 'chosen'? I doubt it very much. If nothing else, for those who are not well-heeled, it can be financially crippling. For those who might say that it *'pays to be Jewish,'* be warned – *'it costs to be Jewish too!'*

I was brought up to eat only kosher food, and I am positive that when I was a child that I thought that all Jews were similarly groomed, which of course is not the case. That was just the way I was conditioned to think as a young lad. We Jews use this endearing phrase '*keeping kosher'*. The word '*kosher*' has been more recently adopted by the English language to mean, in a much wider sense, '*above board'*. It seeks to give any transaction legitimacy. I suppose the inference is that kosher food equates to clean food and therefore, by analogy, kosher business dealings are *clean* ones, if that makes any sense. It was also adapted as an epithet for money. There was kosher money, and then there was black money, according to whether tax had been paid or not. For Jews, the word kosher merely means the dietary laws of the Jewish faith. But, like everything else in the Jewish religion, it is inevitably subject to numerous interpretations. Where I draw the line is far removed from where the frummer from Stamford Hill draws their line. There is clearly kosher, and then there is…even more *kosher*. There is, what is sometimes called *glatt** Kosher. This must mean, as I understand it, that an even stricter rabbi has been supervising the preparation or the slaughtering process. But maybe there is an even higher authority than that – a direct line to God himself perhaps?

The mind boggles at the thought of all these various levels of kosher or *kashrut** (the rules of Jewish dietary observance), every one potentially vying for some kind of monopoly on what Jewish law really means. It seems that every Jew believes that his level of Orthodoxy is right, not just for himself, but for every other Jew in the world.

I never knowingly eat non-kosher food. This means that when I go out for a meal, I never eat meat, other than at a kosher restaurant of which, in Manchester, there are very few. I eat fish, but not shellfish, and yet I eat from the same plates and cutlery on which bacon has probably been served that same day. I look most times to see whether food contains gelatine and if so, I put it back on the shelf because of its animal content. It's all I know. This is the way I have been brought up, and this is who I am. I am a Jew and I feel a strange sense of obligation not to let it all go down the pan. I readily admit that it is, to a large extent, a habit rather than a true religious belief, guilt rather than passion, fear rather than conviction. I suspect that, as well as *Community* and *Continuity*, I must rely upon my *Tribalism* too.

But *why* do I really do this? *Why* do I choose not to eat these so-called forbidden foods, and seriously limit my range of eating habits? Why do I follow these religious rules, whilst disobeying others? Why do I deny myself the joy of eating meat that has not been koshered? Why do I make such a business about *treife** (non-kosher) food, when I am not clear what it is I believe? *Is it all just brainwashing, or does it mean something more?*

When I was young and living in Crumpsall, and in the predominantly Jewish enclave I have already referred to, I remember going to Brundretts, an old-fashioned sweetshop on Middleton Road, just round the corner from where we lived. Here I would buy little chewy sweets, called black jacks and fruit salad. They were four for a penny in old money, and I absolutely loved them. In those days, I never looked to see if they contained gelatine and yet, oddly enough, I would carefully check this nowadays. I am getting worried that maybe I'm turning frum after all. I have always had a real yearning for a fur hat and tights, or maybe not.

I have also never tasted a shrimp or a prawn, so far as I am aware, though I once crunched on something in a soup that had me a little worried. I have done without ham and pork for so many years and so have never felt any need to explore. But why do I deprive myself of the foods that others scoff on with relish, and appear to survive?

The answer to this question goes to the root of who I now believe I actually am. Somewhere in my conscience, maybe languishing in the depths of my soul, there resides a voice that reminds me who I am. I do not hear the voice of God, you may rest assured, but my own in-built set of rules that may be appropriately defined as brainwashing, dictate who I am and what I do. I am no born again Jew, but I was always born a Jew. Out of apparent respect for my parents, who have handed down to me certain of these rules, I eat what I eat, and refrain from eating what they have told me I am forbidden to eat. I call it ***respect***, though maybe it is fear. It may be all of these things, or it might be something else. It might be, for all I know, that God is indeed residing in my conscience and that it is this that determines what I do, and who I truly am.

But I have to concede that there is a genuine, almost obsessive, need for me to hang on to who I am. This does not arise from any religious fervour, but more out of a sense of duty. This is who I am. I have the same sense of destiny as my parents have clearly felt in the past. They handed on to me these rituals, and I now do my best to hand them down to my own children. This is an emotive response to who I am. Something inside me tells me that this is what I am obliged to do. The traditions that I cling onto are not necessarily those directly associated with the small villages of Eastern Europe, but rather more the landmarks of my childhood, the Hebrew songs, the Shabbos candles, the multi-coloured candles at Chanukah, and all those other symbols that comprise the fabric of my upbringing. I remember all the festivals that punctuated each year. Chanukah, Rosh Hashanah, Yom Kippur, Pesach and the rest. They give Jews identity, difference, family, purpose, ***Continuity*** and, once more, ***Community.***

In the Holocaust, Jews of all religious persuasions were, as is extensively recorded, herded together like cattle in their overcrowded trucks. Some lucky ones survived, but not that many. Millions more perished. Thus I feel a deep sense of duty to hand on to my children some semblance of Jewish identity, as it is part of a rich tradition and an important aspect of who I am. I am fearful that if I let just a little more go, I will have nothing whatsoever to hand over to the young ones, and I will have been responsible for destroying my heritage and their hope. I will be guilty of cutting the umbilical cord by severing my link with the past. I cannot do it.

Whilst I may have doubts as to the religious foundation for such rituals, there is still a need in me not to let go. There is something intangible and ill-defined which encourages me to wave the Jewish flag and ensure that I have played my tiny part in ensuring the survival of all those other Wandering Jews, past and present.

So the truth appears to be that I eat kosher food, not necessarily out of any deep-rooted religious belief, but out of a sense of perceived duty, destiny and tradition. I am not sure this makes any great sense to anyone else but me, but it is to the best of my knowledge my own truth. It is a kind of identity or kinship that I am attached to, and am reluctant to let it go.

I am one of the wanderers who may, as I have already admitted, from time to time walk away, but I am also one of those Jews on the periphery who is inevitably drawn back like a magnet to who I am, and to that little part of me I am determined to retain.

I am hesitant to give up on that possibility that **Hashem*** is there after all, seated on his ivory throne, and with a flowing white beard. I am not willing to rule out any possible options. I see signs of his presence in the cry of the innocent child entering an otherwise troubled world, and my hope is literally rekindled when we light the Sabbath candles.

I view with much confusion the endless array of ritualistic customs. At Pesach, as I have previously mentioned, the extended family sits around the dinner table as the youngest child, if old enough to do so, asks the father four questions, the same darn questions each year. I think to myself, if only he had listened properly last year, it might not be necessary to go on repeating the same questions. At Sukkot, a makeshift and temporary hut is erected with a roof that can be removed in order to expose it to the elements and the skyline. We look to the stars and enjoy an uninterrupted passage to the heavens, so that maybe God might look on us benevolently. At Yom Kippur, we fast for more than twenty-four hours, and put on footwear not made of leather. At **Purim*** we are encouraged to drink and be merry, whilst audibly demonstrating our distaste for **Haman***.

I no longer have an intimate relationship with most of these festivals. Even Shabbos no longer represents what it once did for me as a child. I used to go with my father to Whitefield synagogue, where we sat next to one another in the front row, talking discretely, though incessantly. In more recent years, I would take Dalia to the smaller synagogue in the Bowdon assembly rooms near home, where the Lubavitchers had set up home. When I don't go to shule, I do miss it. I value that sense of community, the peace, the hope and the tradition. And the talking of course.

I have only very recently discovered something particularly interesting. We light the candles on Friday night to welcome in the Sabbath, as is the Jewish tradition. As a religious symbol, it arguably might have limited relevance to me. And yet, I look into the window where I see the reflection of the orange flames of those two candles, and I discover a kind of serenity, and even a sense of spirituality. It is as if I am once again crying out to return. I called it before: **Coming home** and, in a sense, that is precisely what this is. Those candles represent peace and calm, and have become a particularly meaningful symbol for me, epitomising tranquillity. I used to invariably wear a suit on a Saturday, as it was my special day. It was God's day of rest and, in an odd kind of way, it was mine too. There was a gap in the week between the start and the end, as against the endless cycle that the introduction of Sunday trading has created in the English world. As the saying goes, '*we need a break*'. My own view is that it was a pity they got rid of Sunday closing, as nowadays the week is continuous, with not a moment's respite.

So here again, I must willingly accept that I am ambivalent. I go along to synagogue at Rosh Hashanah where I find the forced hysteria slightly nauseating, and yet I feel a need to be part of it all. At other Jewish festivals, such as Sukkot or Chanukah, I play no part, and yet I am always aware that these special days are there for me, should I ever want to be part. If I am not there for them, I know that they are always there for me. Take them away, and I am stripped of a further small fragment of my identity. They remind me of my childhood with genuine fondness and are an integral part of my Jewish calendar.

And then there is the Sabbath, supposedly the most important day of all, and a day that regularly comes around every seventh day. I travel in the car, I rarely nowadays go to shule and, though not proud to say it, I desecrate the Sabbath in a most unholy way. Yet Friday night is the night when most Jewish people like me stay at home. I sit down on a Friday night for a special meal, and I look into those symbolic candles that burn so brightly, signifying our long fight for survival as well as the embodiment of Jewish continuity. The orange flame burns, and the Jewish people live on. It is a comfort and a reassurance, and means a great deal to me.

When I speak to a Jewish business colleague in Israel, she tells me that she is not religious at all, and yet she is forever referring to our festivals, and how much she looks forward to celebrating them. I understand all of this, as these festivals are a part of who she is, and who she chooses to be. I have ultimately discovered that the Jewish religion is so much more than a religion. In a curious way, I have concluded that it is just about possible to be religious without believing in the Torah at all. Secular Jews particularly in Israel are constantly reminded of who they are, as the shops close down and welcome in the Sabbath on a Friday night. Meanwhile, the Jews of the diaspora are more urgently reminded of who we are, when we are under threat, when we walk together in times of trouble, or when we celebrate happy occasions.

But the essential question that I ask myself is: **Why do I have such an illogical attitude to these many Jewish beliefs and customs?** There are, I now surmise, a number of possible explanations. As a young boy, the candles were lit, we sat round the table, I went to shule on a Shabbos, I asked the four questions at Pesach, I shook the ***lulav**** at Sukkot, I received my cheder prizes, I sang the songs. These are fond memories for me, and I inevitably reminisce affectionately. The synagogue, in my childlike eye, with its grand and marble stairs leading to the ark, where the Torah is kept safe and adorned in velvet and silver, was a place with which I became familiar. I was with my people who pampered me and who would always look after me. I felt comfortable and no longer lost in the crowd. I was part of something. That something was the Jewish tribe of Israel.

As an adult, I guess that I am just too frightened to let go. I may not be the greatest believer, but I look back upon those childhood memories. There was a sense of order, meaning, hope and civility, within the clan of which I am by birth a member. I read prayers in Hebrew that I do not understand. I sing songs with familiar melodies, but no meaning. I pray to a God who never shows his face to me. But this is what Jews have always done and, though there may be many temptations elsewhere, Jews like me return to our roots. However implausible or fanciful the biblical explanations may be if taken literally, people like me return, as if we are returning home to a place that is comforting and welcoming. Like pigeons, we have a homing instinct, and we fly to a place where we feel secure and which we recognize only too well from our younger days.

In my own case, I think there may be a particular reason for this. This might explain why I feel instinctively uncomfortable in a Reform synagogue, where men and women sit together, and many of their prayers are recited in English rather than Hebrew. Their cars are parked outside the synagogue on a Shabbos though, strictly speaking, we are not allowed to drive on the day of rest. Their rationale is that we need to change with the times and, if we drive to synagogue, why do we need to hide the fact? They argue for transparency and truthfulness, so that Jewish people might adapt to a modern world. For Reform Jews themselves, they make the right decision. It remains their God given right to choose. And they do.

My own emotive response has in the past been entirely different. I do not want my religion to change. I want my religion to be the religion I remember as a child, the familiar prayers, the meaning of which I do not understand, the inspiring tunes I hum to, and the rules and customs to which I have become attached. I want to feel an insider, as against an outsider, in a place where strangers nod to one another, where we talk continuously, where we compare the week's politics and business, and where men sit together in rows, whilst the women are seated in their own section, on the periphery as ever. This is the traditional Jewish way of life, and I am instinctively reluctant to dismember it. It is the continuity with which I clearly identify. I might even be regarded as a traditionalist, rather than a moderniser. Maybe it's just because I am too frightened of change, or it might be brainwashing. But the traditions are what I clutch onto as I reminisce and reflect.

It is a place where belief in God is secondary to believing in this structured way of life, and the determination to see it thrive, despite all threats to destroy it. This is the **Community** of which I have spoken, and which I recall and treasure, as I wander alone around a remote cemetery, honouring familiar members of the tribe.

For me, my Jewishness is arguably the only aspect of my life that never changes. This might finally help to explain the mystery as to why it is that, when I go abroad and frantically search for a synagogue, I feel this huge sense of empathy as I recognize the same prayer books, the same ark, the same bimah, the same religion that has survived worldwide throughout all those eras. When I went to the Ukraine, I saw a synagogue there, just like my own back home, amid the concrete grey buildings of Odessa, with high levels of visible security. I felt an enormous sense of pride, as it proved a common thread. My heritage was there for me to behold in the freezing temperatures of Eastern Europe. I look around a synagogue on a remote Caribbean island, with loose chip stones on the floor, and feel a huge surge of excitement that these too are *my* people, though on this faraway island.

Their Judaism is ***my*** Judaism, their prayers, ***my*** prayers. ***My*** doubts, I suspect are theirs too. We might have our differences, but our history is the same. I have been on a walk-around tour of the shule in Turin, as well as the breathtaking shules in Rome, which the current and previous Popes have visited. They are, in a strange kind of way, a vital part of who I am. My heart flutters because of my sense of belonging. The tribe of the Israelites flourishes in every corner of the world, partially because it has resisted change. In a world where nothing appears permanent, these religious customs and rituals, as well as the monuments that house them, represent longevity, solidity and permanence. Tribal? Maybe. Communal? Definitely. It is all about a sense of belonging, and to witness the Jewish tribe spread thinly across the world, and in remote quarters, can be such an immensely uplifting experience.

Meanwhile, there are many aspects of Jewish religious life that I find particularly difficult to comprehend. As well as understanding the real purpose of vast black hats and long curls, I do find the act of putting on ***tephillin*** * rather curious. A box containing the Torah on my forehead does not always sit neatly with me. Tsitsit with tassels, white tights, even the havdalah candle, and even Elijah supposedly visiting every Jewish Seder table on a Passover night. All these emblems are archaic, hard to accept, and yet part of the story. They are still an integral part of the unchanging landscape to which I have just referred. Each of them, in their own special way, are representative of Jewish custom, and every single one highlights one of our continuing dilemmas, integration and assimilation, and where to draw the line. More to the point, where do I personally choose to draw that line? This is the matter to which I referred much earlier on in my journey. How do we reconcile the right of a Jew to wear a massive hat of fur and white tights with the need to have an inclusive society, where it is intended that we should all integrate?

I had thought, until I started on this momentous journey, that without religious belief, I was not a Jew or, more particularly not a ***proper*** Jew. I no longer believe this to be true. My journey has radically altered my view on this. Being Jewish means much more than believing in an omnipresent creator. Being Jewish means believing in the immeasurable value of what has been created. All these strange rituals, with which I do not easily empathize, are nevertheless a part of my upbringing, and with which I am familiar. Chanukah - with its rainbow coloured candles, Purim and the ***hamentash,*** * and even those bizarre looking chaps always running to shule, armed with their ***tallit bags**** and serious looking personas. It is an undeniable fact that they too are a small part of the person I am today. Their journey may have been a different one to mine, but we Jews have all suffered the same fate and share the same Ten Commandments, however differently we choose to interpret them. If one of us has been chosen, then all of us have been chosen. They have a mezuzah on their door, and so do I. Their mezuzah may be a more expensive one than mine, but I have a mezuzah, pretty much like theirs and with the same purpose. We are part of the same tribe, otherwise known as the Jewish people. We were, and forever remain, however far we may stray, part of that tribe of the Israelites, whether or not I believe in Moses and those bulrushes. I share the same history as each of these boys in the frockcoats, white tights, vast hats and curly locks. Whatever our differences, our route as Wandering Jews is actually remarkably similar. Their grandparents have journeyed from Galicia and the Ukraine, just like my grandparents. They have no monopoly on my religion, as I share it with them too. **They may be right or they may be wrong, but we are brothers, because we are, if nothing more, the Wandering Jews.**

My Jewish faith is a religion that, to a rather large extent, depends upon culture and custom, as much as it does upon the word of the Torah. It relies upon our history as much as it depends upon our future. Nothing that occurs in the future can wipe away the tears of our much-maligned history. That history has moulded us, both as individuals and as a tribe. The notion of the stereotypical Jew can distort the truth, as I have already conceded. Not every Jewish person behaves in the same way at all, but there are certain aspects of my own character that are at least arguably typically Jewish, and it is these characteristics that are a part of my Jewish identity. Our core beliefs are essentially the same. I may personally have more of an issue with believing in God but, like the ultra-religious, I respect my parents, I treat my neighbour as I want to be treated and I even refrain from murdering anyone. I know the difference between right and wrong, no less than they do, and I may even practice it as *religiously* as they do. Our interpretations may differ, but our building blocks are the same. These strangers are part of my extended family, and vice versa. We go our separate ways, but we remain one people. They are as entitled to their Torah as I am entitled to mine, and we have much to share that lies beneath and beyond the curls and the extravagant hats.

It is this history, including the Holocaust in particular, that has helped to materially shape the person I am. It is this same suffering that has determined my attitude to my Jewishness. I hear and read of conflict between one religion and another. I read of acts of anti–Semitism and Islamophobia. I sometimes hear of Jews making distorted and ill-informed statements about Moslems. I am aware that some Moslems express vehemently anti-Semitic attitudes, often linked to Israel. All of this is the continuing story of racial disharmony, hysteria and religious elitism. It is disheartening, but desperately needs confronting. We all have a duty to confront uncomfortable truths.

As I have said already, a real issue is how we address the line between assimilation and integration in this era of enormous challenges and conflicts. I am convinced that everyone should be allowed to dress as they wish, whether a burka or a huge hat or a turban or even green hair or a plethora of tattoos. That signifies the right to practice whatever our religion or our fashion dictates. But with such freedom comes responsibility – a responsibility to integrate, to mix with the outside world, to show respect to our fellow man and to conduct our religious affairs in such a manner as not to offend anyone else. If a man is not allowed to shake the woman's hand, he needs to explain with sensitivity why this is the case. We need to start communicating within our own religions, but also beyond. I am convinced that this is a real challenge for all religions and needs to be addressed with absolute urgency. The onus is upon every Jew to fight injustice wherever it proliferates, and whilst we must maintain our religious affinity, we must at the same time contribute to the wider community of which we are also a part. We cannot turn the other cheek when a homeless asylum seeker seeks refuge in our midst. This is how we reconcile assimilation and integration. We hang on to what we believe, but we are tolerant of one another's beliefs. We contribute not only to our own community, but beyond. In simplistic terms, we start to talk to all our neighbours and break down the barriers that divide us. The ghetto has to be extinguished and the Jews let free and uncaged.

Whilst I began my journey by being dismissive of the frummers walking along the streets of North Manchester with their distinctive attire, I now recognise that they are, broadly speaking, what I am too. I have identified the differences, and our respective approaches to the Jewish faith, but I can now see so clearly that we are all returning to our roots. I revert back to when I was a child, cocooned in the comfort of a loving and safe Jewish family. This is where life at least partially stopped on a Saturday in order to mark out the Sabbath. These times hold fond memories for me and sub-consciously, I return to the comfort, the warmth and solace that they epitomise. This Wanderer returns to his childhood and to his cherished Sabbath candles.

What I have taken much longer to appreciate is that the other Jewish Wanderers, those far more religious than me, take it just one leap further back than me. It is all a matter of degrees, and it is only time that separates me from them, as they return not to Crumpsall, but to Eastern Europe, where they feel more infinitely more comfortable. This is where their community sat together, worked together and prayed together. This is the village where beards were long, coats were black and hats universally furry. This is where there was, I am sure, respect between child and parent, and between one adult and another. This is where females dressed modestly, and where Hashem answered every single prayer. This is the place to which the frummer returns, much further back in time than me, but to a place where he too feels equally at ease. He prefers to let time stop at a time when families looked after one another, prayed to their God three times a day, dressed modestly, and did not expose themselves to the dubious influences of the modern media, and its tasteless incursions. They return to those good old days when Jews had 'faith.' These Orthodox Jews keep themselves to themselves and are, so far as I can tell, at peace with their 'Maker' (as my father always put it.)

It is finally obvious to me that Jewish identity is predominantly a matter of degrees. I go back in time, in a similar way as the more religious co-religionists do but, whilst I go back to my own childhood, they go right back to the days of their grandparents' childhoods. I go back to the familiar territory of my North Manchester childhood, whilst the more religious Jews return to the village life of the intimate communities of Eastern Europe, where their parents or grandparents lived harmoniously with their fellow-Jews. The world of the frummer is another world to mine, but a world that they have not created, and merely one they have tailored to their needs. We all want to return somewhere, to a time well before the hustle and bustle of modern life engulfed us.

Judaism is variously described as a race, a religion, a creed and a culture. Though I cannot positively decipher to what extent it is one or the other, I now positively know that it is much more than just a religion. It provides me with a set of rules with its various scriptures, and an amalgam of customs that never really change. Most Jews hang on, if only out of fear that the alternative will be chaos. We are clutching on to our fragile raft as the ferocious waters threaten to engulf us. To many of us, it is a world that we do not understand, a language we cannot follow, a premise we do not always rely upon, but an ethos with which we are inevitably comfortable. It is this familiarity with our cultural customs that encourages us to remain involved. It gives us both solace and a genuinely comforting sense of belonging.

So the Jew who I find myself to be is not in fact quite as confused as I imagined I once was. I have made a habit of distancing myself from members of my own community who refuse to move on with the times. But I am, in fact, more like them than I probably thought. I too desperately want my childhood back. We have lost something special. We run, but we do not know in which direction or to what destination. There are so many choices nowadays, and so we become increasingly confused. There is so much immediate knowledge at our fingertips that we are at risk of becoming brain dead. For every step forward, there are two more in reverse. We cure illness. We create stress. We create endless choices and we become increasingly confused.

As I delve a little deeper into my own inner self, anxious to discover what my Jewishness honestly is, I discover an inner calm. My journey has hopefully taught me to be more tolerant of every shade of Jewish belief. I understand the importance of tolerance towards all people of any belief, or not. We all of us need to integrate by talking, by educating, by embracing difference, rather than being intimidated by it. A black fur hat is a black fur hat nothing more - and it never attacked or insulted me. A burka is a burka and harmed no one either.

Whilst I find my own comfort in the Shabbos candles, the next Jew feels a need to wear his Jewishness on his sleeve, or on his head. The Orthodox Jew expresses his Jewish identity by returning to another world. His vast hat encircled with fur might look unconventional, but it expresses who he is. He chooses his own time warp and feels secure in his own place of safety. We are all of us searching, but in our own particular way.

Some days I am *too* Jewish, as when I choose to go to Auschwitz three times, not just once. Other times, I am arguably not Jewish enough. But the fact remains that, whether I am the Hypocritical Jew, the Apologist Jew or merely the Secular Jew, I am the Jew. I was born to be a Jew, and I shall be a Wandering Jew for the rest of my days. And wherever it is that I shall wander to, there is something inside me that summons me back to the community of which I am a definite part. It is the Jew in me. Take that away from me, and I am empty, devoid of soul.

Out of an inner sense of destiny, duty and commitment, I cannot let go of that baton that has been ceremoniously handed down to me, in order that I may pass it on to my children. Drop it, and I am out of the race altogether. Hand it over, and I give my children their own choice, the very same choice I once had. Perhaps this is what is meant by that term **Chosen people**. Not so much that we were in fact the Chosen ones, but the ones with the important choices to make. Not that we were the objects of choice, but *with* the choice. A choice whether we wish to ensure the community continues its journey or not, and whether our continuity has any true value, and is therefore worthy of preservation.

And so this sometimes-weary Wanderer returns. I value the traditions and the customs more than I probably ever appreciated. I respect the sacrifices others have made on my behalf. I accept who and what I am. I have identified some of the common themes of my own Jewish identity; **Community**, **Continuity** and **Custom.**

I am English by birth, a fact of which I am proud. But I am Jewish too. I can be both, and I am both. But being Jewish is at the heart of who I am, and hopefully determines the way that I behave. I am striving to live a life that encourages assimilation and integration as partners in the ultimate creation of a fairer society.

And, most of all, my inner Jew tells me – Never ever give up on *Hope*.

- **MATZO** is an unleavened flatbread that forms part of the Jewish festival of Passover (Pesach), and now available during the year. The matzo is a symbol of 40 years in the wilderness where the Israelites had to leave Egypt so quickly that they had no time to prepare the food for their journey, and ate an unleavened version of their customary bread.

- **CHAMETZ** is what the Jewish religion forbids us to eat on Passover. It literally means 'leaven,' as against matzo, unleavened. More particularly, it means any food that is made of grain and water and allowed to ferment and 'rise.'

- **BETH DIN** is a house of judgment and the rabbinical court of Judaism. It also is responsible for supervising the Jewish dietary laws.

- **GLATT KOSHER** is used to denote stricter standard of Kashrut (see below)

- **KASHRUT** is a set of Jewish religious dietary laws and ensuring the food is kosher.

- **TREIFE** simply means food that is not kosher

- **HASHEM** is one of the Hebrew names for God, though, in prayers, God is expressed in Hebrew as 'Adonai.'

- **PURIM** is a Jewish festival commemorating the salvation of the Jewish people in ancient Persia from Haman's plot to destroy all Jews, young and old.

- **HAMAN** is the main antagonist in the Persian empire, determined to see the annihilation of the Jewish people (see Purim above)

- **LULAV** consists of branches of palm trees and is one of the four species associated with the festival of Sukkot.

- **TEFILLIN** are a set of two small black leather boxes with straps worn by Jewish men during weekday morning services and containing parchment with verses from the Torah.

- **HAMANTASH** is a filled pocket pastry in a triangular shape usually associated with Purim, and containing poppy seeds.

- **TALLIT BAG** is a bag, often of velvet, in which the tallit, or prayer shawl, is carried.

CHAPTER NINE

THE PRAYING JEW

'Friendship. If not for ever, then for what?'

- **MILTON FIRMAN**

'My God, why, oh why, do you make life so immensely difficult for me?' They say that you revealed yourself to Moses, apparently handing him two awesome and formidable tablets with some well-constructed commandments etched upon each of the stones, and yet you seem so obstinately intent upon avoiding me altogether.'

'I can appreciate the good sense of what is written on the stones, but why do you never take the time to explain their meaning to me face to face? 'Why?'

'Surely, it wouldn't actually be so terrible, would it, for you to turn up one day at a party or in the park, if only to free me from this eternally mysterious, guessing game? You appear to derive some kind of perverse satisfaction in leaving me in this eternal limbo. You want me to find faith, and yet you seem to do everything possible to hide yourself away, by placing obstacles in my path. When things go right, I have to assume that you're behind it, and yet when things go wrong, it is always human error. God's will – or not, and all that jazz. Come on, you have to be a little more realistic than that. If you are so damn clever, then show me.

'If I am blind to you, is that entirely my fault? Surely even you – if you can be objective just for one single second – can visualize my turmoil? You can make my life easier if you really want to do, as you are apparently omnipotent and omnipresent. If not you, God - then who? It's all this mystery that I can't get to grips with. I can see no logical reason for you not coming down from your ivory tower, if only once a year - when deciding who by fire, or who by darn pestilence and the rest.'

'And I must now confess, were you to ever seriously appear before me, I have stored up, over endless years of soul-searching and torment, a number of really important questions, of which the following are just a few random examples. So here goes. Sit tight.'

'What is this business about - never showing me who, or indeed where, you are. Yes, yes, …yes - I know all about miracles, but as far as I am concerned, it would be a miracle if you just winked at me with one eye, in order to let me in on this great big secret of yours. You surely know me well enough by now that I can be relied upon to keep a secret. You could just show up one night as I am sleeping, and curl up next to me, or you might even show me a small sign – perhaps by solving the Middle East crisis at a stroke and thereby saving a heck of a lot of suffering. When all is said and done, it was you who created me. Well, wasn't it? If not you, then who? Yes, I know that you created paracetamol in order to provide some relief, but why ever put me through this dire pain in the first place? Yes, I know what your good book says – trust me, but why should I trust you, when you desert me in this quite merciless way?'

'Sometimes I really think that even you don't begin to fully understand my dilemma. For all your wisdom and creativity, I suspect that you too can miss the obvious staring you in the face. Is it really any wonder that I am so confused? Yes, I know about the womb, but I can't really say with any certainly where I actually came from, or why I am really here, or where I am bound. What sort of mind game is this that you play? Why not just put me out of this purgatory? Forgive me for saying it, and I do so with genuine respect, but I think it's quite unreasonable of you to expect me to have faith in you, when you give me no clues. Some days, there actually appears to be no purpose at all, as none of what we see or hear lasts forever. If I truly believe what the bible says, then I eventually return to dust. This is all very benevolent of you. You sit there in your grandiose tower, somewhere faraway in the distance, possibly above the clouds or even on Saturn, knowing full well that my life is not eternal. That I am mortal. That I will die. That I will be forgotten by future generations. I try to understand the purpose of spending six arduous days creating something that breathes and exists,

only then at some unknown date in the future to stop functioning at all. This is all your handy work. To me, it sounds absurd, and yet you have the audacity to call yourself - a friend, even a Father – One in whom I am expected to have unflinching faith. I am supposed to believe that Moses got the tablets, Noah - the boat, Abraham - the lamb, and David - the Goliath, but why should I believe any of these fanciful fairy stories?'

'I am supposed to pray to you a certain number of times each day in order to offer my thanks - to worship you, to marvel at you, and to regard you as the all embracing, the ever loving Paternal One. But if you have the power, then kindly explain - why did you create such conflict and misery? If I have a choice, what about you? Did you not have the ultimate choice as to the type of world you wanted to create, and the character of its temporary guests?''

'I do not, in any respect at all, demean the manner in which You give me eyes that see, ears that hear and hands that touch, but only then to make them all dissolve into nothingness seems positively bizarre. Tell me – what's the point of all this? I know I am only human but, by my simple reckoning, it all sounds perfectly daft and pointless. You may not know or truly appreciate this, but we humans, well certainly most of us, pray for some measure of immortality, without which life appears to be transient and futile. We say 'forever,' but we know it never is. It is all very unsettling. I suppose you've heard of Dawkins who says that you are nothing more than a delusion. I hope he's wrong. But is he?'

'You must surely recognise the logic of what I am saying. You see absolutely everything, and so you must be aware of exactly what I am thinking. You created our minds and our thoughts. There is an element of futility to all this life that apparently you have single-handedly created. I know that you must see this. I just know you must. Yet what do you say? Nothing, as always - absolutely nothing. Forgive me for saying this, but you can be so utterly frustrating when you never answer. I cannot see you. I cannot touch you. I cannot hear you. But the question is – can you hear me? If you can, are you listening?'

'And now let me share with you something else that I also find particularly troubling. Even if I accept that you, alone and unaided, created this world, why create evil too? You are God, a name which I have always assumed is, in effect, a pseudonym for goodness. So why create the evil of the devil? Surely it makes better sense to create shades of goodness, rather than to introduce evil into this already over-complicated and complex equation? But I can see – as I again anticipated, that you say nothing, absolutely nothing. You leave it to me to ask questions, and then so frustratingly, I must try to answer them myself. Yet you know, in your heart of hearts (should you have one), that I am in no position to answer these questions. Tell me – is that fair? Why do you put all the onus upon me?'

    'Is there some spiritual benefit in leaving me in turmoil? Is this your mystical way of ensuring I suffer, so that I might appreciate happiness and fulfilment in the next world? I must admit that I think suffering is awful and needless, and I am desperate for your explanation, not your infuriating silences. I need you to talk to me, and help me to rationalize it all, and yet you leave me in total darkness. I hope you don't think that I am being disrespectful because I am, in fact, in fear of you. But why should I have faith in you? Have you automatically gained my respect, or do you need to earn it? The tsunami definitely wasn't my doing, or the earthquakes, or the widespread famines, or poverty, or the floods in Haiti or Pakistan, or the typhoon in the Philippines, or illness, or injustice, or disability. OK, I know perfectly well what you will say, and you may well be right, that human beings have made a hash of the earth that you created, and so it is we who must pay the penalty. But it was you who gave us the choice to abuse the environment, and it is you who can surely put a stop to needless suffering. Is it any real wonder that I am so cynical? You may have a different perspective than me with your Godliness, but surely even in your eyes, (should you have those too) you can recognize suffering when you see it?'

    '**You must be fully aware that when those horrendous and vicious waves that you alone created rose up and crushed the flimsy buildings of the Far East, they were destined to cause immeasurable damage and suffering, even to those who survived their mighty onslaught. The innocent. Lifeless. Homeless. Parentless. Totally destitute. Is this your idea of a fun day out on Boxing Day? Or is this something else that I haven't quite grasped? Does this needless suffering serve a Godly purpose that I am as yet unable to comprehend?** I know full well that you will have anticipated that I will raise with you the distressing and sensitive topic of the Holocaust, which frankly I am loath to do. It is the question that every Jew inevitably asks. **How could you, the powerful, the forgiving, and the righteous one, allow this mass murder and annihilation of the Jewish people to go unchecked for so many painful years? You ask a Jew to shovel the body of another innocent Jew into a corpses pit - was this your idea? To allow one Jew to prepare another for his degrading demise in the ovens of a death camp? You want me to pray to you, to thank you for such dastardly things, or just to have faith in you. But there are, as you well know, many more atrocities that you have allowed to happen. You have** allowed human beings to descend into the depths of depravity and to abuse one another. Rwanda, Serbia, Zimbabwe and all the rest of the locations across the world associated with demagogues, pillaging and dehumanization. I know you have your reasons, but more the pity that I don't know what they are, and nor can I understand how anyone who can seemingly put a stop to this, allows these acts of God to happen year after year, when desperate and innocent people cry out for your help. And you serious want me to have faith in you?'

'As I have indicated, I have questions, indeed crucial questions to ask you. Firstly, I must confide in you, and you alone, that the question that bothered me most of all as a kid was, where did you come from? In other words, can you tell me, who created you? This troubled me when I was a youngster, and you will know full well that it gave me a headache, and yet there was still no answer to be had. As an adult, I tend to think about it in terms of timelessness, but this is merely a mechanism to contrive an answer of sorts. So level with me – who was there before you? If there is a reason you cannot tell me, then just say so, but don't leave me in this tortured state of turmoil a moment longer. I am a big lad now and I can deal with whatever your answer may be, even bad news. If there is a reason for this bedlam, then speak to me now loud and clear. I need your reassurance, love, meaning and purpose. You tell me that I am your offspring in your image and so I plead with You – show yourself to me, and put me out of this endless, pitiful misery.'

'My God, I can similarly understand what a tremendous job you have done – creating an entire world in six days. That was no mean task at all, and more than fully deserving of a prolonged rest on the seventh day. I gather you had no help, so hey, hat's off to You – very, very well done. I hand it to you. If ever there were a true miracle, then that would have to be it. The creation of the world – Wow! What did you have before you created the earth, and what came first? Why a sun, a moon, a donkey and a fly? Surely it would be no less a miracle if I were to know how you did it? This is a miracle, not magic; you are God, not David Blaine, and so let me in on your secret please, and reply to that one question, the answer to which has eluded me for all those years – *what came before you?*'

'The rabbis tell me that I must believe, and they urge me to find faith. But why should I have faith in You? You must play ball with me too and help me just a little tiny bit. I hear of 'Born again Christians' having a sudden vision, but, strictly between you and I, am still waiting for mine. I gather that you know everything. I don't wish any of your many believers harm, but I do actually suspect that it might well just be a case of self-induced hope over faith, rather than any real apparition. I would never wish to undermine their faith, and the journey they took to discover it. I admit to you, and you alone, that I remain sceptical. Can you see that? Please don't be hurt, and start writing my name in the strangulation Book.'

'Don't be angry with me for saying these things to you, as I have no desire to be on the wrong side of you – Mighty One. To be perfectly honest, I have already admitted that I am actually quite nervous of ever offending you. I hear of some of the things you can choose to do to me - famine and pestilence, and even water or fire. I cannot pretend that I am not a little tentative, and maybe that is the way it is meant to be. But I can think of better ways to die than through lack of food, or being strangled. Can you provide any reassurance? No, I don't suppose you can.'

'So there you have it - you probably knew what I was going to say anyhow. I often wonder whether I have a choice at all, or whether I am pre-programmed by you. If you are truly omnipotent, then presumably you have not only created me, but also dictate how I behave. It is not that I am angry with you, but just a little frustrated to say the least. '

'Another thing before I go. There are believers of all creeds, and even sub-divisions of each creed having their own versions and blends of religious observance. Christians, Moslems, Jews and the rest. We pray towards Jerusalem or Mecca or even Rome. We wear small hats, big hats, silk robes, black robes, white robes or no robes at all. We burn big candles, small candles, or no candles whatsoever. We worship Mohammed, Jesus, Moses and Buddha. Some pray on Fridays, others on Saturdays and others on Sundays. Some pray in English, others in Latin and yet others in Hebrew. To whom are you listening? For once in my life, just tell me - who is right - and who is wrong, or are we all right? Level with me now. Is this a huge practical joke? You can tell me if it is. Is the truth that we are all wrong, and that we get what we see? How can we all be right?'

And then it appears that in every single religion, there are numerous interpretations: celibacy, women priests, literal interpretation of the Torah or the Koran, and then that old chestnut - Jesus Christ. Some of us say he was a good Jewish boy, a good man and a genuine believer. Others believe much more than that, and adhere to the principles of the Christian religion. They say that he was crucified on the cross and then rose from the dead. As you know, though I personally don't go for it, Christians and others celebrate Christmas, and then Easter, in deference to Jesus whom they claim is your son. But we Jews are told to believe otherwise. Now, let's have this right – either this is or it isn't the case. It is a very easy question for you to answer. Yes - or No? Both of us can't be right. They are so convinced that they are right and they would, if given the chance, convert me to Christianity. They are convinced that Jesus is your son and they want me to benefit from their spirituality. If they are correct, it is better that I know right now - and I can put the Torah back into storage, and get across to a cathedral right now and bend both knees in Christian prayer. And whilst this particular argument rages, there are other religions subscribing to their own versions of the bible. As you will probably know by now, there is an Old Testament and then a New one. There are churches, synagogues, temples, chapels and mosques, all professing their unique route to their Maker. Are they all right, some right, or none of them right at all? If you are receptive to prayers, do you have any preferences? Hebrew, English, spoken, sung or just well intentioned? In a group, or on our own? Three times a day, five times, ten times? Or just maybe – not at all. What's your preference, sweet Lord?'

'I appreciate that I am asking a whole stack of questions but, as I have already told you, I have had so long to store them up for you. Yet another matter that troubles me greatly is that I am informed that you apparently chose the Jews, so the good book says, but explain to me – if you really did, then for what reason? Is it a privilege, or a burden? My concern is that the mere reference to one group having been 'chosen' has led to much resentment over the centuries among other religious groups. I understand this very well. For someone to be 'chosen' implies that someone else has been left out, and that can't be that fair. But was this your choice of word, or someone else's? You may be able to understand why I am so bemused by these various beliefs, seemingly all legitimate in their own way, yet at the same time at odds with one another, sometimes literally in conflict with each other. Not only, as you of all people know, are we at war between one religion and another, but as between one faction and the other. Was this your bright idea to have so many religions? Surely one God, one belief and one religion would be perfectly adequate. What do you think?'

'To me, it seems sufficient to have the ten commandments, so why introduce a mammoth 613 rules for every aspect of Jewish life? What is your view? I have expressed to you in absolute confidence how confused I truly am. Yet I then look at what I witness on a daily basis. I see childbirth, the natural growth of vegetation, the sun's orbit, the intricacies of the human brain, the mouth that eats, the eyes that see, the nose that smells. These are the miracles to which I have readily referred. Maybe you are right after all. I just need to have faith in you. Maybe you are right. Maybe. But only you know.'

'And this is just part of the problem – what do I know? What am I supposed to know? I listen to the 'Today' programme on Radio 4 and I hear the former Chief Rabbi, a formidable orator, a believer and an academic. He seems so utterly convinced by you, so why do I not understand where and who you are? If he can see you, why can't I? It is easy to put it down to superstition, but I feel guilty when I doubt you. I speak to you, though you do not respond, and I even pray to you, if only when things get really sticky. I look, but I do not see. I see, but I doubt. I feel, but I do not touch.'

'But I cannot, and will not, say you are not there, in the distance perhaps, looking down and keeping us safe after all. I do not want to ever reach the stage where I have no faith in you at all. Not to believe in you is tantamount to believing in nothingness. I want to fill the void in my life with some substance, meaning and purpose, and desperately want to believe that this huge, expansive world was created with an order, and an overriding dream in mind. To condition myself otherwise is to be doomed. With real *Hope* in my heart, I reflect upon what you have allegedly created and, with due humility, I try to give you the benefit of the doubt. I take a fresh look around, and I see rolling hills in all shades of green, a turquoise bloom blossoming in springtime, and a petite, dainty red robin with his colourful, red brushed breast returning to nest. I munch on a juicy apple or a crunchy carrot, and I look up at a moon suspended in the sky with no strings attached. I witness the seasons, the autumn shades, the winter crispness and the magic of the summer sun on the rare occasions it shows me its face.'

'But even more breath-taking is the mystery of life itself. In a quiet moment, I ask myself what greater wonderment can there be than the complexity of the human mind spawning great academic achievement, the seed of sporting accomplishment, or the portal for literary prowess. Every creation evidences a different face, a unique body. Each person possesses their own character with emotions and thoughts, identical to no one other than themselves. The beating heart, the rate of the pulse, the smile, the tear, the scream, the compassion, the memory, the vision, the love, the devotion. Sight, smell, touch. All the things I tend so freely to take for granted. But no more.'

'I must believe that there is a purpose to this life, a benefit that I cannot recognize from suffering, and a vision of a God I have never seen, but whose creations I witness every day. I am not ungrateful, though I admit to being lost.'

'You say precisely nothing. This is the mystery of life itself, and I have to live with that realization. Hopefully you will have your reasons for remaining so ominously quiet. I think I have understood that by now. And I live in constant *Hope* that you are here in residence, that you are a compassionate God, not over-troubled by who prays and who does not, but accepting human frailty and rewarding goodness and substance rather than my empty words.'

'Thank God for that at least. Maybe one day, you will talk to me. But not today. It might well be that the answers I am desperate to find really lie within. I see your miracles, so why do I need to see the One who created them. I very much *Hope* you're right, and that one day soon, I will hear your voice. Until then, my Lord, rest assured, I have just written a book, as you presumably already know, and I have discovered two things. Firstly: The answer lies within. And secondly, I have found *Hope* - and I fully intend to hang on to it. In the interim, should you ever be in the area, do call in. You will be made most welcome.'

I may not have seen you, but I have seen the results of your hard work, and I am genuinely impressed.

CHAPTER TEN

THE WANDERING JEW

"Hence today I believe that I am acting in accordance with the will of the Almighty Creator by defending myself against the Jew. I am fighting for the work of the Lord."

- ADOLF HITLER

So, here it is, the question that I inevitably and eternally ask myself - do I actually believe in God? How many times in my lifetime have I repeatedly posed this question? Now I have had my head to head conversation with God – the question still needs to be asked: **Do I truly believe in God?**

Five simple words - five words, but with a complexity of meaning almost beyond human comprehension, and sufficient to make my head whirl in a frenzy. Once I knew, now I am not even half sure. Do I believe in God?

For me to attempt to answer this most fundamental question of all, I need to be clear in my own mind as to whom or what God truly is. The preliminary question has to therefore be – **What do I understand when I refer to 'God'?**

God is by common definition regarded as the Creator of the universe. Whilst interpreting the bible literally or not, when we refer to God, we mean the Creator or the creative force that caused us to be here on earth at all. We may call Him by different names, Allah or Hashem, God or the Lord, or some other chosen name, but I suspect that most of us are, in actual fact, referring to one God. By God, most of us refer to the means whereby we were created. We may, as individuals or individual religions, claim the monopoly upon Him, and declare some divine right to possess Him, but the presumption is that God has no brothers or sisters. God is one. God is good. Is that the inference I am entitled to draw from the name we have given to Him?

I have sometimes raised an interesting rhetorical question: Why are we so certain that there is only one God, and would it be such a very bad thing if there were, in fact, two? Maybe my God has a brother who also has creative powers. I must add that I am not wishing to be disrespectful or flippant when I ask this question but it is in my opinion a perfectly valid question.

Those who are believers commonly reject the notion that we evolved over the millennia, by big bang, or by any other scientific means. Those who believe in God must also surely believe that the Creator created the world for some meaningful purpose, whatever that precise purpose might be. The eventual conundrum might well be that we cannot truly understand who God is because God is the very essence of life's existence. He is the mystery itself. For me, I believe that this is an inescapable truth. We are searching for the intangible and for a Faith we cannot touch. This will surely be why the phrase '***Blind Faith'*** has evolved.

A belief in God presumes an objective, an order, and a meaning. But then, like any obstacle race at a long-forgotten school sports day, there are many further hurdles to overcome, some particularly demanding and very awkward, yet frequently overlooked. To merely record the fact that I believe in God fails to address that preliminary question:

Who is my God?

Is He a God who created this world in a brief number of days, and then waved a fond goodbye? Is He, as the bible would have us believe, watching over our every move? In other words, do we have what we regard as free will? Is He omnipotent and omnipresent? And, even if this is the case, how does this impact upon our daily lives? Is my perceived choice in fact, ***His*** choice? Am I in fact ***His*** servant, and no more than an automaton, rather than a freethinking person in my own right? I have often pondered the extent to which I have 'free will'. I even think the phrase itself might be a misnomer.

The fact that we might be willing to accept that God created the world does not necessarily establish that He is an entirely Good God. I can look around and see much evidence to the contrary, human suffering and acts of God, resulting in further widespread and life-changing destruction and misery. The sun, water, hurricanes and money are far from evenly spread across the world's disparate peoples, with a consequential undercurrent of inherent injustice. People in all quarters suffer through no fault of their own and they, in particular, must see little sign of God's great gifts amid their own drudgery.

The fact too that He was the Creator does not necessarily mean that He is necessarily the listening God. There is a God, and then there is a bible, and there are prayers, rules, regulations and yet more rules, all confined to one religion or another. But does a belief in God, a Creator, presume that I must also believe in all the baggage that comes with Him?

Can I have a God without a religion? Can I have a religion without the institutions? Can I have a religion without a God? Can I have a God who does not hear my prayers? Is there more than one route to God? Can I be a good Jew, but believe in the Christian God? Does my God have to be a Him and not a Her, a grey beard rather than short back and sides? The mind truly boggles at the questions that need to precede the seemingly straightforward question: Do I believe in God? These questions reverberate deep into my eardrums.

Does my God have to be the one who parted the Red sea and who single-handedly delivered the Ten Commandments? Or can I simply say that I believe in God as the Creator? No more. Not necessarily ubiquitous, but simply the Creator. The miracle maker who caused plants to grow, animals to feed, humans to procreate, and waters to ebb and flow. That would surely be sufficient? If I believe in this, then I must surely believe in God. I would be able, within that context, to equate nature with God.

Maybe my God is someone who was just handy at building worlds, like some others might be good with plasticine, or balsa wood. He builds people and worlds, rather like Rupert Murdoch built businesses.

It now appears to me that the question that I have been asking myself over several decades, as to whether I believe in God, is a particularly naive question; it fails to address the core issue. There is a substantial enough challenge believing in someone I do not know and whom I have never met, but the greater barrier is that God can be so many things to so many people. I need to struggle with my own personal dilemma – **Who** is God? More to the point - Who is *my* God? In simple terms, what does the term 'God' mean to me personally and arguably just to me? In order to be consistent with the thrust of my personal search, I must define 'God.'

One of the fairly obvious questions which arises is whether I can be Jewish without believing in God. Can I believe in a different kind of God than the one who created the world in six days, brought us rainbows, punishes those who disobey Him, and is ultimately He who always knows best? It is little wonder that, faced with such hugely complex and demanding questions, my head aches and I become prone to sinking under the weight of such a heavy burden. I also obviously respect the fact that this is an onus we all share. The conventional image of God is that of a male, rather elderly, grey haired, kindly and benevolent who sits aloft on a rather grand throne, and is referred to sometimes as the King of Kings. He is visualized as the One who created everything, from the cow to the flower to the monkey to the soil. This is what God is – the ultimate creator of everything I see, I touch, I hear and I feel. What face I put on Him is secondary to the concept that God is the answer as to how we apparently came to be on this earth. He is the creator of Adam and Eve, and every single one of their descendants. He is the answer to the mystery of Life itself, and is the personification of that mystery.

But who is God?

Who is this person or thing or body or entity that apparently single-handedly created this entire world, and where did He himself come from? What motivated Him to create the world with all its apparent imperfections? This is that old chestnut that bothered me indeterminately as a child and even now, after so many years, still preoccupies me. I am a pragmatist, and I accept the fact that there will presumably be no composite answer to this most fundamental question in my lifetime. I must persevere, and so I do, by asking other question that similarly appears to be relevant and pressing. In order to ascertain whether I believe in God, I must investigate *who* God is. If God if my maker, I can live with that. I see childbirth, flowers, water, earth, fire and wind in abundance. These are all someone's creation, not mine, and not yours. I am content to describe these things as miracles. I can find no logical explanation, and so they are by my own definition miracles. They form the backbone of what I have just termed – the mystery of life.

But beyond a basic belief in God as the Creator, what else am I to believe? Must I believe in the Merciful One, the Listening One and the Gracious One? To believe in God, must I believe in just a Jewish God or a God for all men and all seasons? Do I necessarily believe in Him any less if I do not accept each single word of the Old Testament literally and verbatim? Must I pray if I believe, and if I pray, must I pray morning, day and night? Do I have to believe in every facet of Jewish ritual and teaching for me to be truly numbered among the sons of Zion and a true believer? To be Jewish, need I believe in a particular type of God? Or am I Jewish, if for no other reason than I am born Jewish? What does my Jewish identity demand of me?

As I have travelled through life, well before this journey began, I never gave much thought to this process, and the various aspects of religious belief. I appreciated that there were rules that governed our actions, and that helped to define our level of religiosity. However, not until I embarked upon this personal and gruelling journey, did I give real thought to the underlying issue as to who my God is, and what I must believe in order that I might say that: ***I believe in God***.

Of course, I have heard many a Christian say that they regard themselves as religious, and that they pray, though not in a church, where they regard the institution as irrelevant or out of tune. In the Jewish religion, there is something else of consequence to consider. Praying should be undertaken, according to Jewish law, within a communal setting, and should ideally be in a ***minyan****, in effect a congregation and quorum of at least ten men of post-bar mitzvah age. To pray in isolation is a lesser form of prayer, as I understand it, and the corollary to which is that the synagogue becomes a vital point of reference where we pray, and where we are encouraged to pray in the company of our fellow Jews. We truly fulfil the mitzvah of prayer when in the company of other Jews.

I have alluded to the concept of **Community** as a central theme of Jewish life, and this is exemplified by the notion of a minyan. It is a religion dependent upon a communal setting, and a kindred spirit. The community is its lifeblood - and where the Jewish pulse pounds.

But I consider momentarily whether I must do more than to believe in my Maker, in order to qualify as a Jew. I ask myself a series of self-searching questions. ***If I believe but do not pray, am I not a Jew? If I pray, but not in a minyan, am I not a Jew? If I pray even in a minyan, but I am not sure if He actually answers me, once again, I ask, am I not a Jew?***

This is my dilemma – where do I draw the line?

These questions go some way to explaining why religions such as Judaism become so fragmented. There are numerous shades and degrees of belief based upon our personal interpretations. There are Jews who believe that God was the author of the Torah, and they interpret the Jewish rituals literally. There are others who accept that there is a certain gloss put on the biblical tales of heroism and devotion. There are others who call themselves religious Jews, but regard Judaism as being fluid, and of necessity moving with the times. Each Jew has his own slant, his personal definition and his own interpretation. There are believers, and there are **believers,** just as I explained with grades of kosher food.

In Judaism, there are the **Hasidim** with their black coats, enormous hats and white tights, whom I have mentioned already. There are **Lubavitch**, the 'new boys on the **black**', representing a slightly more modern traditionalism. There are Reform, Conservative and Liberal Jews. They comprise every possible shade of theological thought, yet all within the general framework and loose definition of what we refer to as, 'the Jewish faith'. We are all Wandering Jews.

Jews like me are born to be Jews, because this is who we are. But what we as individuals mean by the term 'being Jewish' can differ from one family to another, and one individual to the next. It seems to me that I can believe in God, but not believe in another person's definition of who their God is. God is in truth who I believe He is. He is more a concept than a Living Being. We create our own vision largely based upon our rather restricted human experience. I suspect He may not have a beard after all.

I ultimately conclude that I can believe in whatever aspects of God I choose, and only then am I able to say whether I do actually believe in God. There must be times (I think to myself) when even a Chief Rabbi or an Archbishop has moments of self-doubt. I want to know who his God is, and whether my God is his God, and whether 'my' Jewish is 'his' Jewish.

I tried to speak with Him but He did not answer me. He has nevertheless left his mark. His miracles are here on earth for me to behold. I do not take them lightly, and nor do I underestimate the clear evidence of his fine work. I see it daily. I witness life in its full glory. It is too easy for me to become complacent, but these are the miracles on full display for all to see.

And so ***If not Him, then who?*** If not ***Hope,*** then what?

He has produced to me these incredible and inexplicable miracles on earth, and yet I demand more. Why should I expect anymore? If I see a wonderful sculpture that only one artist could conceivably have produced, do I really need to see the sculptor? And if I do not see him, does that mean the work of art he created no longer exists? He has made my heart beat, without which my life is totally extinguished. I have no other explanation for this. This is the miracle.

I have therefore eventually recognized who my God may be. He is the inanimate force beyond my own limited understanding, responsible for creating life itself. I have no pre-conceptions as to what form my God may take, but I am tempted to humanize Him as we all do, in order that I may personalize my relationship with Him. I can only try and visualise Him, if I can compare Him with someone or something with which I am familiar. He may be a He or a She or may be neither. He may be on a throne, or a stool, or neither. I suspect I shall never discover anything more regarding His true identity. I have never seen Him, and frankly I don't now expect to do so. But what I can see is his fine workmanship in the shape of life's miracles. A have witnessed Life itself – God's greatest miracle.

I am satisfied that He was the Creator. My God is the Creator or creative force who created nature, the birds and the bees, courgettes and tulips and all the rest. They are the miracles I desperately look for but which I can witness for myself every day. Life itself is that miracle. The child. The tree. The flower. The fish. The mammal. The brain. Need I look further to find the miracles of the Creator?

They are God's conversation with me. It is the miracles that speak to me, rather than the voice of God itself. The miracles that I frantically seek out are in fact staring me in the face, as I witness the plant growing out of the soil, potatoes from the compost, and the baby from the womb. Even if the Red Sea was not parted or the animals did not exit from the Ark two by two, the indisputable fact is that life itself is the miracle. It is that which I cannot explain in purely human terms and is, by its obvious nature, extraordinary. Truly beyond any words I can find in my own vocabulary. I might not accept Jesus Christ or even my own prophets, Elijah and the rest, but I see what I see, an amazing world – a world full of mystery, and I witness the miracle every day of my life.

Accordingly, it appears that I believe in my own version of who my God is. My version may not satisfy the frum Jew, or the Pope, or even my own Chief Rabbi, but my interpretation is presumably as valid as theirs. I believe in miracles if only because I see them every single day of my life.

My God is what I cannot understand or touch or see, but whose magical work I can marvel at every day. Need I say more? Need He?

My God is here and there, as was always claimed, in the distance. He is the one with sole possession of the mystery as to *why* I am here, *when* I am here and *where* I go next. There is hopefully a purpose, though I have no idea what that purpose may be. This is the mystery and this is where my God resides. I am hoping that he is the embodiment of goodness - but I cannot be sure.

Does He listen? I have no idea. Is He a Merciful God? I hope so. Do I have faith? I will never give up on trying to discover it. My God is in the cry of the baby, as well as in the ovens of Auschwitz. He is the life I do not understand. I must believe that He is the One, the only One who knows life's true purpose. If he has a brother after all, then so be it. But I have to conclude that Life hasn't just happened.

My understanding of who my God is permeates my Jewishness and my Jewish journey. I think about Him frequently, and even I turn to Him from time to time, though generally at times of selfish desperation and dire need. I hope that He is there to assist the Helpless. I hope that He is a good and caring God, and that he has something better in store, beyond that desolate cemetery to which I will return once more.

I do not know the answers that the serious looking man with the shtreimel on his head has discovered, but I shall certainly never give up on *Hope*. I have not given up on Him being out there, though I cannot pretend that I know.

I feel as if I have grown up as I have journeyed. I have thought a great deal. I have sought many answers. I have tussled and I have struggled. But at the end of the road, I have found *Hope*. Though I now believe that I will never know for sure, I go on hoping. I see life and nature's treasures, and I have good reason to *hope* that God has his purpose, and yet sees no reason to reveal that purpose to me just yet. But I can still go on hoping that he will do so one day soon. I shall never give up on *Hope.*

If my journey has given me nothing else, at least I have discovered that one precious thing. *Hope*. I may not have heard God's words, but I have certainly witnessed his work every single day of my life.

- **MINYAN** is a quorum of at least ten men over the age of 13 required for traditional Jewish worship.

CHAPTER ELEVEN

THE JEW WANDERING HOME

"There are two lasting bequests one can give one's children. One is roots – the other is wings."

-   HODDLING CARTER

When I embarked upon my journey more than three years ago, I never thought that it must end in the very place where it had begun, in the same cemetery where I had wandered so long ago, close to a busy motorway, yet in a lonely, deserted, silent spot. But this is where I have felt compelled to return. This is the place in the country where, as you will recall, my late father, maternal grandfather and grandmother, an aunt and an uncle, among so many others I once knew so well, ended their lifetime days. This is the destination of their final journey, and where my own journey began. This is the place to which I now return, in order to complete my often emotional and highly charged sojourn of Jewish self-discovery.

I feel at this precise moment a compelling and almost uncontrollable urge to revisit this saddest, yet possibly the most uplifting place of all, in order to rediscover not just where I embarked on my journey, but to reach out for that peculiar and intangible spirituality for which I seem to eternally cry out. This is a special opportunity to quietly reflect upon my journey with you, and my search for the real meaning of Jewish identity. I return in the knowledge that, since my last visit, I have looked inside my heart and mind, and wrestled with my own conscience, in order to find and define the real Jew in me, and to discover where my real Jewish identity truly resides.

At times it has been painful and frustrating and at other times inspiring, as I have travelled to all corners of my mind. I have confronted truths and desperately sought answers. I have not knowingly cut any corners. I have confronted God – face to face. I have faced my own hypocrisy. I have tried my best to unleash the truth.

Today, I return to the cemetery in order to doggedly look at myself, and to discover what I have learned about my concept of 'Being Jewish'. I wander among those tombstones once again, in order to reflect upon my personal life's journey and to consider what, if anything, I have learned about myself, and in particular, about the Jewish bit in me. I return to my roots, and to the cemetery's overgrown weeds that I remember so well. I wonder what three years hard labour and honest thinking has revealed about me, and to me.

It is with some trepidation that I methodically and strategically place my rather tatty, crushed, plum-coloured velvet yarmulke in the breast pocket of my suit jacket, as I dutifully prepare for the last leg of my memorable journey of solitary contemplation. The Jewish Wanderer returns home once more to his people, armed with a few carefully selected white and shiny pebbles to be carefully placed upon gravestones targeted by me for this purpose. This is destined to be one day of profound insight and reflection for me.

I am nearing the end of this particularly circuitous road, and on this momentous occasion my eyes fill up with tears to the point of imploding. I ponder long and hard upon the self-reflection of the last several months, and I lay my hands on my siddur, clutching it nervously as I prepare for my return. I go armed with my kit – my yarmulke, my siddur and my ubiquitous handkerchief. I know what to expect, and I go as fully prepared as possible.

On this auspicious day, the sun is again shining brightly, casting a long shadow, as if to acknowledge my homecoming. I stop my car conveniently close to those same big black entrance gates. This is my déjà vu moment. I spy a battered and grubby Volvo motor car this time, parked immediately in front of my vehicle, and I assume that there are other rather more religious visitors here today. But still totally alone, I take an involuntary and pensive gulp, and embark upon the lonely trek up the stony incline to where the tombstones are laid out in their sometimes orderly but clinical fashion. They are positioned just where they were last time, but with a number of new additions, being the shinier ones of the recently deceased. I am nervous, though I am not sure why. This is where I started thinking hard about my Jewishness, and this is where this illuminating journey will end – marking the end of life, and the end of my eventful and purposeful journey.

My heart is weighed down with the burden of mixed emotions, as I am brought back down to earth once again in this place of stark finality. I wander once more in total silence slowly and deliberately along a particular row where I see an inscription I had been sadly anticipating after my last visit. Jeremy's stone has now been erected since I was last here. **'Aged 51'**, it reads: *'a dear husband and father'* – this is where my cheery old school pal is finally cast in stone. I remain with him for a few quiet moments, putting one of my cleanest pebbles down at the end of his headstone, and promising him that I will return to see him again soon, and so I will. I speak to him as if he is still here, when the fact is that I know full well that his heart stopped beating some considerable time ago. He had waited his turn but in the intervening months since my last visit, his stone was laid, and there is now a token reminder of Jeremy, recognizing the fact that he had once walked on the earth that I am currently but temporarily occupying. He exists in my thoughts only. Pleasingly, there are many pebbles on his tombstone. He was once a popular young man, and I am relieved to see that his memory remains dear to many. I can hear his contagious laughter in my imagination, but I now regret that I never told him whilst he was still with us, how much I liked him. Yet another missed opportunity, one of many in my lifetime thus far. The number of pebbles tells the story. He is loved a lot, and rightly so. I shall go and see him again soon, as I promised him. And a promise is a promise. I hope he can still hear me.

As I place the pebble on that gravestone, I think of those buried here who get no visitors, and not a single stone, and I cannot help but feel sorry for them. The pebble is there if only to tell the world that they will not be forgotten. That someone misses them. And yet time passes, memories fade, and pebbles no doubt get fewer and fewer, or are even become displaced. Even the cemetery is not for ever.

By this stage, I am in pieces as the customary barrage of familiar names comes flooding back yet again. Once more, I read the names of friends of my parents, once pillars of the community, but now only pillars of salt and grain and dust. Several old friends of mine, as well as some young children who were deprived of life so soon all lie beneath ground - prostrate and helpless. But on this occasion, I take some lingering moments to carefully read out to myself each single inscription, and then to place a small stone down to record my visit and my everlasting bond with each one of those departed. I lay stones where there are none, so as to try and ensure no one is left entirely alone. How sad this all is. I think *'hope'* to myself as my only means of confronting this rather shocking reality.

Odd though it might be, I place more emphasis today upon these religious rituals than I did the last time I was here. Everything has somehow taken on a different meaning for me, though I cannot explain exactly why. These rituals, out dated, outmoded, pointless, make me hang on to my precious ***Hope***, and thus serve their purpose. I have learned to be more tolerant of my own people, and their various and varied beliefs.

I now, a little begrudgingly perhaps, accept that these rituals are significant aspects of my life and that the Jewish customs, whether partial superstition, brainwashing, delusion, belief or mere tradition, are an important part of my Jewish identity. I am acutely aware that the journey that I have taken has brought me back to this bleak outpost, peppered with black, grey and white granite, where I had embarked upon my travels, armed with endless questions as to who I really am. This is the location I felt compelled to return to, in order to ask myself where I had reached on this journey of mine. It is its' tradition, its solemnity, its calm and its complexity that brings me back home. It is familiarity – the names of those I once knew, and who are all part of a clan – ***The Wandering Jews***.

Today's piercing sun does nothing to conceal the pervasive sadness, and the all-encompassing and chilling stillness that permeates this remote cemetery. It is just as I remember it, predominantly desolate and eerily quiet. It is a monument to a Jewish community that speaks of the past, though makes no sound. It is a place for thinking a great deal, putting life in perspective and accepting life as it is. An opportunity to pray for more and to *hope* for meaning.

I have a number of specific gravestones to visit, but I am distracted, as I make my way through the long, unkempt grass. I see some black hats in deepest prayer in the distance, and assume, probably correctly, that these are the unnamed occupants of the Swedish car that I had seen parked near the entrance gates. These men and women are seriously at prayer, rocking back and forth as religious Jews are prone to do and probably entirely oblivious to my presence. I marvel that their God apparently accompanies them even to the cemetery, whilst my own thoughts drift elsewhere.

I am wearing my yarmulke once again out of tradition and respect, rather than as a sign of any newly discovered religious fervour. Though I brought it with me, I actually left my siddur in the car and rather than praying, I am initially driven by a sense of duty and commitment. I immerse myself in private thought and contemplation, rather than any formal prayer or messages to God at this special time. I have done my talking to Him for now. I need to do a little more pondering.

My father's stone stands proudly as always in a row to my left, and alongside are many of his contemporaries whose names I recall very well. Many of these people were once great, certainly to those who loved them, and yet now they are merely fond, distant memories in a mind's eye. The granite has weathered well, and I know that my father would be pleased as punch that I am here with him once again right now, honouring his memory and the treasured aspects of fatherhood, and our special friendship.

As I stand before him, my mind turns to those yesterdays. I think of brown cornets from the ice-cream van on the way to Blackpool; the sand dunes at St Annes, armed with my plastic bucket and spade; playing the drums, as I feebly accompanied my father's vastly superior piano playing; singing in the shule choir, as dad conducted us with customary vitality and aplomb. I think back to the two of us having a private joke together that only we two fully understood. But, most of all, being father and son with one another, whilst not knowing how short-lived that privilege was destined to be, both for my father and his son. Irreplaceable. Entirely and utterly irreplaceable.

Though I am not certain it is what I am meant to do here, I feel suddenly compelled to spontaneously recite the kaddish – possibly because I know dad would have liked me to do that. I need no siddur, as I can recite it from memory, despite it being in Hebrew. Tears stream down my face as I mumble the words out loud, and pay homage to my dad. This is the same memorial prayer that Rabbi Marcus had recited at Auschwitz, and for me right now it symbolises everything I am. I thank God in the prayer but I am in fact praying to a father who was my special buddy and who through no fault of his own, left me to grow up without him. I wipe away my tears as I re-read the inscription that I have read numerous times before: '***Jack Firman -who died the 13th February 1979 remembered by…***and so forth' I will not accept that this is it - the end of everything. And so, more than ever, I hang on to my precious ***Hope***. The last bastion.

I spend a few more moments, frozen in time and in deep thought and intermittent grief. I am whimpering like an injured animal in this faceless place. I reflect upon what I have learned in these intervening months, and acknowledge to myself that a certain part of my Jewish identity resides in this particular place. This cemetery, with all its confusing signals, is itself part of who I am too. I feel close to its symbolism and its traditions. But most of all, I feel close to all those with whom I once shared my daily life. When we had arrived in Whitefield, there were only about a dozen Jewish families in the area. Years later, there are hundreds upon hundreds as the community grew from its tiny acorns.

In the row where my maternal grandma and grandpa are buried, there is now a new joint gravestone in black polished granite, bearing the names of Harry and Terry ("Tilly") Baker. Auntie Terry was the personification of tenacity, but even she could not hang on until I had finished writing this book. In her last days, I never heard her complain once, and nor did anyone else to my knowledge hear her raise a single grumble. I now have two grandparents, together with an uncle and an auntie, by strange coincidence, all buried alongside one another in one fairly neat row. As anticipated, auntie Terri joined them shortly after my first Chapter was written, and the dancing did finally stop, like a strike of lightening, her dancing shoes destined for someone else's feet, though I know not exactly whom.

I place my pebbles down, one on each stone, grandma, grandpa, uncle and now – aunt. I feel sapped, and yet strangely rejuvenated, in the company of fond and cherished memories. I pay my own restrained tribute to their memories. This I realise is the heritage that I will hopefully hand over in due course to my children, for them to make of it as they choose.

After wandering around totally alone some more, I walk away in pensive mood, and in the grip of an almost inevitable melancholy. I catch sight of yet more names I recognize, one after the other after the other, and I cannot help wondering yet again what this is truly all about. When I see a gravestone of a four and a half year old child I never knew, I am shaken - and I crouch down to place my final pebble on this tiny, tiny tombstone, and then am forced to look away. I have had quite enough. I have seen too much today and I am crying again. It is time to leave.

As I cautiously depart the cemetery by those huge black gates, I turn around and utter a reluctant and rather feeble prayer to my absent God.

'Please God' – I plead silently, and with fragile and flickering sincerity –

'Let there be a purpose to this, even if it is one that I do not comprehend. Please let there be some meaning to this chaos. Let me hang on to my Hope.'

Unsurprisingly, and a fact to which I have become accustomed, I get no answer, none at all. But I have learned in the last months an important truth – *The answer lies within.* **Whatever my beliefs were, I have come to understand that, as long as there is life, with all its miraculous manifestations, I am bound to hang on to my** *Hope*. **It is that** *Hope* **that sustains me. Were I to forsake** *Hope*, **I would be left a broken man. This is one of the essential things my journey has taught me.**

I finally leave, though somewhat sluggishly but with renewed purpose, heading towards the entrance. I screw up my yarmulke. I didn't need my siddur after all. My tissue meanwhile is its soggy self again, as it was always destined to be.

As I leave alone and immersed in self-contemplation, I finally accept that the Jewish religion is only one aspect of my own Jewish identity and that ritual, *Culture*, common ancestry *Community* and *Continuity* are collectively at the very heart of who I really am. This, I believe, is an unusual aspect of my 'being Jewish'. Religion can, and often does, play second fiddle within my own Jewish experience. Being Jewish is much more than banging my chest to demonstrate my faith to all the other congregants looking on.

Even when strict religious belief is wavering, I am – I now know, beyond any real doubt, positively immersed in my Jewish identity. It is who I am, not even necessarily who I always want to be, but who I actually am.

And to a large extent, the other *C* represents the *Choice*. It is the choice I do not have. Born to be a Jew, I am a Jew. Religious or Secular, Orthodox or Reform, I am Jewish by birth, and there can be no escape, even if I wanted to find one. This particular *C* signifies the choice I do not have.

Through a process of *Conditioning, Culture, Community* and *Continuity*, I have imbibed the customs and rituals of the wandering Israelites who have suffered together, often perished together, but ultimately survived together. I may doubt our legitimacy. I may decry or doubt the teachings of the Torah, but these other '*Cs*' enable me to retain this deeply instilled sense of identity. I am hooked on my Jewishness as if I am suspended on a clothesline. I am linked to a religion that I never fully understand, but which claims to understand me.

Jewish by birth, Jewish by habit, Jewish by manner and Jewish by *Community*. Like many others before me, I may have wandered, but I inevitably wander back home, returning to where I unavoidably and indisputably belong. As to the Jewish religion, my journey has reinforced my own beliefs. I acknowledge that life is a mysterious journey and with no definitive and earthly answers. I have eventually accepted the fact that there are huge gaps in my knowledge and understanding, and each of us has the right to fill that gap with whatever we choose, Atheism; Orthodoxy; Agnosticism, self-doubt or faith. The fact is that this remains the ultimate battle between despair and faith, *Hope* and resignation. Scholars and academics will differ as to where life began, but I have finally resigned myself to never knowing. Call this defeatism, but this is where I am. I now acknowledge – Acceptance. *Hope*. Optimism. Mystery. I witness daily miracles, such as childbirth, and remain hopeful that there is an overriding purpose I am unable to fully understand. I am filling this huge gaping hole with *Hope,* without which there is a real threat of chaos. But it is a *Hope* not founded on desperation, but on strict logic. I might not be able to prove my God exists, but the corollary is equally true – I cannot possibly prove He doesn't exist either. And so I retain the *Hope* that indeed He does. And as long as I go on witnessing miracles, I will go on retaining my precious *Hope*.

As to the other elements of my Jewish identity, each plays a vital part in defining exactly who I am. These are the aspects of Jewish life that prompt me to seek out Jewish places of worship in faraway lands and assume an affinity with a spoon bending Israeli whom I had never met before. It is these aspects, collectively and individually, that cause me to stare into the flame of the Sabbath candles and dream of fulfilment, peace and tranquillity. **The Jewish Sabbath is a part of who I am too. I do not honour it as I should, but I celebrate it. It symbolizes the same *Continuity* and the survival to which I have regularly referred during the course of the journey we have shared together.**

The element of *Community* is an integral element of what I have discovered myself to be. I often claim to be an isolationist or even a recluse, but I delude myself. As with many others like me, I might enjoy my own company, but I also recognise the huge benefit of being part of a community. *Community* provides me with a sense of belonging to an ethnic group into which I was born, and itself held together by custom and ritual that form my bedrock.

I recognize artefacts and symbols of Jewish ritual that I can sometimes too readily deride, but nevertheless still treasure. They too, a little like the pebble on my father's gravestone, mean something personal to me. They are part of my community, and I am part of them. To Jews like me, community is important if only to underscore a sense of kinship and purpose. Contrived though it may be, this sense of allegiance, generated by the notion of community, is an essential aspect of my own Jewish identity.

Conditioning is the term I apply to describe what others may call **nurturing**. I adopt the word, not necessarily in a judgmental way, but to signify my weakness and my human fallibility. I have to acknowledge that I have been conditioned by my Jewish upbringing. I have been conditioned to think and react in my Jewish way. It is all a part of the bigger picture, and an essential ingredient of my persona. I have been conditioned to be proud, defensive, apologetic, passionate and Jewish, whatever that all means, and in whichever order of priority. This amalgam of characteristics and influences is part of my Jewish identity. I have been conditioned to do my bit to ensure the survival of the Jewish people, and to encourage my own children to marry within the faith. Nurturing, conditioning, brainwashing, call it what you like, but I cannot deny its intrinsic influence. I have mixed in Jewish company, laughed at Jewish jokes, and cried at Jewish misfortunes. This constant exposure to all things Jewish is bound to have influenced me, and to have had a lasting effect upon the person I now am.

The term *Jewish Culture* is really an anachronism. When I have been to the ballet, I rarely see any Jews either dancing, or even watching. We are not renowned for being opera buffs either. But this is not, actually, the culture to which the word *Jewish* is applied as the epithet. *Jewish Culture* is more a way of life, to which I have frequently referred during the course of my journey. It includes the Jewish festivals, Jewish liturgical and other music, Friday nights with the family, salt beef sandwiches with *latkes**, human suffering, and charitable contributions. These many facets of what I refer to as Jewish culture are nothing more than aspects of traditional Jewish life. Like Yiddish, these various aspects run through my veins, contributing in no small measure to my Jewish identity. I sometimes want to let go, but I have no real choice. They are all an integral part of who I am.

The notion of Jewish culture is closely related to the concept of Jewish community. **It is our common culture, familiar rituals and Jewish customs that collectively create the cherished Jewish community.** It is the community that offers Jews a sense of cohesion and belonging, and helps us to achieve a collective identity. We are part of a relatively small community, which does not evangelize, but rather creates barriers to membership. It is a culture that discourages inter-marriage, if only because that threatens to undermine our Jewish continuity. This community is undeniably part of who I am. In my hometown, this community has its own home for the elderly, social services, hospital visiting service, day centres as well as youth groups. It has developed its own established infrastructure that seeks to uphold the essential Jewish tradition of caring for one another. This is the exemplification and the embodiment of the Jewish principle of Community. And it is a part of Being Jewish that makes me so proud.

If the community, culture and even our conditioning have a value then the lifeblood of the Jewish people is worth preserving. For me, it is this notion of longevity and continuity that symbolize my life's true meaning and purpose. In other words, though I am bound to accept my own mortality, my legacy to my own children is what I define as the underlying worth of Jewish values and rituals. It is what I am able to pass on to the next generation.

My desire to encourage *Continuity* is sporadically demonstrated by lighting the Shabbos candles, slicing the crusty *challah**, the knotted bread we eat on Shabbos, or singing the Jewish tunes and prayers, all part of what I hand on to my children. Taken in the round, they represent *Continuity* and a positive rebellion against human transience. I have to hand over a baton of Hope at the very least, if nothing more - *Hope*.

The Holocaust only served to make Jews like me more determined than ever to preserve our threatened heritage forever. There is no stronger emotion than the quest for self-preservation and survival. The idea of *Continuity* is therefore at the very root of who and what I am. I am totally dedicated to be the victor against our oppressors, and to encourage the survival of the Jewish nation as a people and as a community. This is an emotive response to who I am, as well as the driving force underpinning my hatred for all forms of racism of whatever kind.

It is perfectly clear to me now that my Jewish identity is a combination of Community, Culture, Conditioning and Continuity. They all contribute to the rich tapestry of my own Jewish life, with all its blemishes and imperfections.

When I began this journey, I thought that I might discover neat answers to complex questions, simple solutions to seemingly insurmountable dilemmas. The fact is that I have discovered something entirely different. The Jewish religion encourages us to ask questions. Each question leads on to another question, rather than any clear answer. I accept this as an inescapable fact of life.

My journey has taught me that there is no shame in not knowing but rather the shame is in not asking, or pretending to know what I do not in fact know. I have learned and accepted that for me personally there is no definitive explanation as to how the world was created, but I recognise that there is an abundance of evidence of both the mystery and the miracle for me to behold. *Life itself is that miracle and I need look no further.*

Whilst Professor Hawking might conclude that he knows the answer as to whether God was the creator, there are many more like me who are far less hypocritical than some young daughters might think. We just don't know how this world was put together, or for what precise purpose. People like me may not have an unfaltering faith, but what we do have is *Hope*.

My own view is that there is nothing disingenuous about this. It is an honest admission that I have not yet seen that so-called light. It is, in my own view, perfectly reasonable to occupy this middle ground, as I am finally relaxed in the knowledge that I will probably never know how life truly began. I accept what I do not know. I acknowledge that I must learn to be more tolerant of others within my own faith, as well as those of other faiths. My Jewish Culture, Community, Conditioning and Continuity collectively enable me to live a Jewish life, as I choose.

I do not know the answer to the primary question as to creation, and it would be churlish of me to pretend otherwise. I *Hope*, but I do not know. I also willingly concede that having been born into a Jewish family, I have no real choice. I may be in denial regarding aspects of the Jewish religion, but my heart is beating to the Jewish tune, armed with its enormously rich culture and precious heritage.

Being Jewish, in the widest sense of the term, is intrinsically the person I am. The wanderer returns home where he belongs. Being Jewish is multi-faceted. Being Jewish is about the life I lead at every turn. To strip away my Jewish identity is to remove my pulsating emotions, my passion, my sensitivity, my questions, my frustrations, and the essence of my Jewishness.

I cried into Alfie's chest. I wept at the Wailing Wall. I howled at Auschwitz-Birkenau. I wept at the Jewish cemetery in Whitefield. Why? Because I am Jewish, and I am moved by all aspects of human suffering as this has been the story of the Wandering Jews.

I am still left with the one profound dilemma that I highlighted at the beginning of my travels, namely the line between assimilation and integration. This is the issue that causes me the most angst, and is the question that necessarily should trouble our world as much as any other religious issue at the current time. It is typified by the burkha, the turban, the shtreimel, and all the other items of distinctive apparel that set apart one religious group from another. Religious tolerance is under real threat as political disputes cause religious divisions, whilst religious fanaticism causes disorder and mayhem. There are serious divisions in our world, and many wars seemingly closely associated with one religion or another.

And so it is that I return, eyes wide-open, to Leicester Road where, you will recall, women are covered from head to toe, and their accompanying daughters are clad in their modest, trailing, dark-coloured skirts. This is where men carry huge prayer books, and, a little defiantly perhaps, dress in their distinctive garb. This is where everything appears in monochrome. Among strict Moslems and Orthodox Jews, we go on building our own ghettos, though now of our own volition. These enclaves need not be any form of bar to co-existence. Whilst we need not assimilate, we must learn to integrate and be part of the country in which we live. This is, for me, the issue yet to be confronted by politicians, religious leaders and the people themselves.

My Jewish identity dictates that I mix freely with people of all beliefs, whilst never concealing my Jewish identity. This is what I refer to as the ***delicate balance***. It is in reality a *'trade off'* between strict orthodoxy, and living in a modern Western society. One person's right shall not unfairly impinge upon the next person's liberty. The religious Jew must surely show the same respect for a non-Jew as for a fellow Jew, for woman as for man, and for back as for white. My personal Jewish identity reconciles these issues by occupying the middle ground. To do otherwise is a risky business.

The Jewish Orthodox chap with the huge black fedora and fringes may be accustomed to turning away from the young attractive female, but the risk in doing so is that, in a Western, secular society, this can so very easily be misconstrued as sheer ignorance. We all have to start talking, and there has to be a new injection of tolerance on all sides. That is why I too need to embrace difference, whether in Brooklyn or Bury New Road. It's a two way street and we all need to learn tolerance – within and beyond our own religion. No one needs to be intimidated by the other person's clothing. And I refuse to be for a single moment longer.

Some of the greatest Jewish leaders of my time have not confined themselves solely to Jewish life, but have contributed equally to the wider community that has, after all, offered Jewish people a refuge from persecution. In my own hometown of Manchester, the late Sir Sidney Hamburger was one such notable Jewish communal leader, renowned for supporting many Jewish and non-Jewish causes. He was involved in heading up the local Health Authority in Salford where he lived, and where he successfully built bridges of mutual respect and understanding among all religious groups. He was Mayor of Salford at one stage too. Local historian Bill Williams, whom I had met many times, and for whom I have great affection, wrote a biography of Sir Sidney, and I went along to the book launch at Waterstones at the time. I politely collared Sir Sidney after he had spoken in his customarily eloquent and dignified manner, and I had to tell him how much I admired him for one particular quality. Even though he did not know me or even know my name, he would always *'nod'* at me whenever we saw one another. When I told him this, I swear to you – he nodded, and then he next asked my name. He was a true gentleman - and I think of him frequently, and with profound admiration.

Whilst always proud of his Jewish roots, wearing his yarmulke at all times, Sir Sidney was a person who stepped out of the ghetto, and reached out to the wider community, to whom he was indebted, and of which he was also part. He struck a balance between his own religious affiliation and the indigenous population, and to my knowledge gained the respect of all who had the privilege of knowing him.

My final *"C"* must therefore be - **Compromise**. This is the only answer to fundamentalism – the acceptance of the other man's route to his God.

I go to the desk at the petrol station to pay for my fuel. The young lad behind the counter is Moslem and he smiles at me. I purposely enter into some harmless banter with him, and I make it known to him that I am Jewish, and that we are brothers. I am yet to meet a single Moslem who has ever taken issue with my fraternal greetings. I ask every one of these young men to spread the word, and I am sure some do. For me, this is an integral part of what being Jewish means to me. Whilst the politicians speak of wars and conflicts, aggression and divisions, I regard it as part of my Jewishness to learn from our own tragic, Jewish history. We need to all start building those proverbial bridges, both within our own religions and sects, and well beyond. And, I remind myself that it is all a question of what we actually do, rather than just speaking about it. As is often said – Action, not Words. I agree entirely. As God himself demonstrated. He was of few words, but his actions have been truly awe-inspiring. I try to follow his example, as best I can.

And so I finally reach the end of my long and fateful journey. I have discovered what I do not know. I have found my Jewishness in all its facets. I have realised that what I once derided was in fact part of me too. I have learned to embrace the Jewish rituals, the festivals and the ultra-frum members of my clan. I have found much

solace in accepting that what I have found is *Hope* – Hope that the miracle of life has an eternal purpose. *Hope* that there is a Creator, and *Hope* that there is a true purpose to our lives. *Hope* that one day soon we can all embrace difference, and learn to live in harmony. *Hope* that the end may not be the final ending, and that our understanding of everything is limited only by the constraints of the human brain. I have learned much more about the nature of my own Jewish identity, and my will to ensure that the Jewish people survive. I crave for mutual respect for one another and our fellow man.

If that isn't Jewish identity, then what is?

It is the *Hope* that manifests itself in all aspects of Jewish life. It is that *Hope* that ensures that the Sabbath candles burn brightly. It is that *Hope* that I pass on to my children. It is that *Hope* that avoids hopelessness. It is that *Hope* that sustains me. It is that *Hope* that gives me self-perpetuating *Hope*.

Purpose. Meaning. For me, a life without Faith can still be absorbing, frustrating and testing, but a life without *Hope* is one without purpose and is actually almost unpalatable. **To be Jewish means to me that I have a desire to keep those Sabbath candles burning in the hope that the Jewish nation, not just its religious customs, but its sense of community, continuity, conditioning, charity and culture all survive for future generations to make the choice.** To carry on, or throw in the towel, just as a defeated boxer might do.

My journey is about to end, though the Jewish journey shall continue, with or without me. I will go my own way now but armed with the benefit of a little more knowledge of who I believe I am. A little Jewish lad from Crumpsall, not that bright, always inquisitive though, generally well intentioned, a bit of a cry baby, but always trying to be a better person tomorrow. Slower than ever now to sit in judgment on others.

But also now more determined than ever to *never* give up on the *Hope* that God is out there somewhere, wherever that somewhere may be, and that there are things we will grasp one day leading us ultimately to the true meaning of life.

And I have similarly understood that the real answers to the mystery of Life lie within.

And that the miracles we desperately look for are in fact always here for us to behold, actually staring us in the face. The trees. The bees. And life itself, in all its glory.

Hope. Now I have found it, ***I will never let go because this is what being Jewish means to me.*** It might not be Faith, but for now it will have to do.

My final words I say with tears in my eyes:

Am Yisrael Chai, which roughly translated is:

The people of Israel live on. We Jews have survived. We have survived by hanging on to what I have been looking for: **Jewish Identity**. It is far too rich, far too complex and far too precious for me to ever give up on it.

- **LATKES** are potato pancakes, shallow fried, of grated potato, flour and egg flavoured with onion or garlic. Yummee!!!!

- **CHALLAH** is a special ceremonial Jewish bread enriched with eggs and generally of a knotted shape (though I don't believe the shape is a pre-requisite.)

Printed in Great Britain
by Amazon